COSTUMES AND SETTINGS FOR HISTORICAL PLAYS

Volume 2
The Mediaeval Period

COSTUMES AND SETTINGS FOR HISTORICAL PLAYS

JACK CASSIN-SCOTT

Volume 2
The Mediaeval Period

B T Batsford Limited London

© Jack Cassin-Scott 1979

First published 1979
ISBN 0 7134 1704 8

Printed in Great Britain by
The Anchor Press Ltd,
Tiptree, Essex
for the publishers
B T Batsford Limited
4 Fitzhardinge Street
London W1H 0AH

CONTENTS

INTRODUCTION

Crown c 1272

Crown c 1307

This second volume in the series *Costumes and Settings for Historical Plays* deals with the period 1200-1550, divided into three sections: Early Gothic, Late Gothic and Renaissance. Collectively, these represent probably the richest period of costume in European history; the gulf between rich and poor was wide, and those who could afford it spent large sums of money assembling extensive wardrobes of sumptuous clothing. Materials were varied and beautifully produced; skilfully tailored and ornamented with fur and jewels they made up into some of the most beautiful garments ever worn. In dressing the plays of such an age the costumier has an unrivalled opportunity to create, where appropriate, magnificent effects and rich displays of pageantry.

However, it is important first of all to remember that the task of the costume designer is to reinforce the dramatic tension of a play with carefully chosen wardrobes. Costume makes a powerful visual impact which must never be underestimated and ill-chosen garments can actively hinder the efforts of the actors and actresses to express the characters which they play. This should never happen — the costumier has to ensure that the players are dressed in such a way as to give visual emphasis to their personalities and moods, to reflect not only their characters but their inter-relationships. This is a subtle and difficult art and is beyond the scope of this book, but I hope I have emphasised sufficiently how important it is to give careful thought to the way this is to be achieved.

The costumes illustrated here are taken and redrawn from various sources and therefore show how the subjects were seen by the artists of their times. For the purposes of the modern theatre, it is invariably impractical and unnecessary to replicate the costumes in every detail; the expense alone is likely to be prohibitive. It is better to consider how a

6

costume represents the spirit of its time and to attempt to reflect that spirit in the reproduction. Shapes and silhouettes are important in this respect — the Early Gothic period was one of long flowing gowns and loose clothing, but by the Renaissance, the easier lifestyles of the wealthy allowed many to consider how the shape of the human figure could be altered and emphasised to appear more pleasing. Tight jackets and waisted gowns revealed the interest in the tailor's art — the dandy was a distinctive feature of the times. The peasant classes, on the other hand, shared little in these preoccupations. Their costume changed little throughout the period covered by this book. Simplicity and the absence of sophistication are charactistic features of their lifestyles which contrast completely with the life of the court. To give an idea of these cultural factors I have included a brief, general introduction to the civilisation of each period although these are not substitutes for the wider knowledge which can be gained from selective reading of historical reference books.

The temptation to be over-elaborate should be resisted. Strive for effect through the contrast of bold colours and shapes which suggest the costumes really worn — if this is successfully done there is no need to spend a great deal of time pursuing authenticity in every detail.

The choice of costume will in part be determined by the settings and obviously these must combine with clothes to support the particular interpretation of a production. The designer-costumier will be guided in this by the requirements of the producer and director, and must always be concious of the need to subordinate visual effects to the drama itself.

I have tried to present the description of the costumes in a straightforward way, but the intricacy of many garments has obliged me, in the text, to reduce particular styles to their essentials and to shun complicated descriptions. This is especially so in the case of headdresses and the more intricate gowns of the later periods. In such instances I have indicated the basic styles which prevailed, and left the illustrations to show how these were elaborated upon and ornamented in the originals. This is true of all the illustrations; I have not attempted to simplify their appearance in the sources, for ultimately it is these original representations which form the costumier's most important works of reference.

The value of constant reference to paintings, sculpture, statuary and literature as source material is fundamental

The square fashionable silhouette of c 1530

Court dress c 1272

to successful costume design, and should always supplement the use of any guidebook. There are many good reference books available which cover all the variations and details which can be introduced to give interest to individual garments. Most costumiers will find more than enough in their national galleries and libraries to occupy the time they have available for research.

The chapters on properties and settings are intended to provide an introduction to the main concerns of the property master and set-designer in working on productions from these periods. The greatest efforts of the property department will be in providing suitable equipment for knights and soldiers. This is no mean task, for the accoutrements of war in mediaeval Europe were complicated and often extravagant, and it is probably wisest to apply limited resources to the production of simple but realistic arms and armour.

The musical instruments I have mentioned will very likely have to be borrowed or hired. If they are unobtainable it is better to do without them than it is to replace them with modern instruments which will surely be only too obviously out of place.

When setting out to costume a production, however big or small, assess the resources at your disposal and keep within their limits. Aim to design and costume the play simply yet confidently, bearing in mind the need to remain at all times in the service of the drama itself. You will find the work satisfying and rewarding.

THE COSTUME

Early Gothic 1200-1350

At this time Europe was a collection of independent kingdoms and states, beginning slowly to escape from the hitherto powerful influence of Roman civilisation and to establish themselves as separate nations — France, Italy, Spain, England and the Holy Roman Empire (Germany). English possessions in France led naturally to a close link between the two countries, and hence to the establishment of international communications between England and the rest of Western Europe. Influences on European costume came from farther afield too — the religious crusades brought about an interchange of Eastern and European cultures, supplying a new range of materials for the tailors of the Western world.

European civilisation of this time was dominated by France, under Louis IX (St Louis), and fashion in particular was guided by French and Italian modes. There remained throughout Europe a degree of uniformity in styles which only later developed into marked national characteristics. The nobility, used to a feudal social structure, enjoyed the best of the available materials but servants and peasant classes had to make do with sober fashions which had little in the way of decorative extravagance.

Increasing trade within Europe, and between Europe and the Middle East, brought about the rise of a class of merchants whose new-found wealth stimulated the economy and allowed more people to enjoy material goods. In some countries the rivalry of the middle classes was deliberately suppressed with laws which allowed only the nobility to wear the most expensive furs and ornaments, although this was rarely as effective as it was meant to be.

In Germany and Italy, the preponderance of small towns and city states permitted a greater degree of freedom and

Judge c 1410

9

Man in short hip-length tunic
with shoulder cape and hood
wearing a high hat with a domed
crown and turned up brim
worn over the hood. He is
wearing close-fitting hose. A
young girl on the left wearing
a short embroidered surcote over
a long kirtle. Her hair is loose.
(c 1307)

rivalry amongst the people, and affluent folk could well afford to vie with one another for the lead in sartorial elegance. It should be remembered here that Germany did not exist as a nation at this time. The Holy Roman Empire comprised several small states — Bohemia, Saxony and Austria amongst others — which enjoyed relative autonomy from one another.

European civilisation was based on a synthesis of Greco-Roman, Christian and Germanic influences, its literature comprising epics, dramas, romances and the songs and tales of the troubadours. Spiritual life was of fundamental importance — church influence was strong in literature and all the people, commoners and nobles alike, enjoyed the religious plays and pageants which were performed in the churches, streets and market-places. As a result of cultural and courtly influences there arose a taste for elegance and style which can be seen in the fashions of the period. Although the cult of romantic chivalry contrasted sharply with the realities of feudal life some of the people at least were now enjoying a lifestyle which gave more time for leisure pursuits and the cultivation of an interest in graceful customs and dress.

This elegance of fashion was most noticeable in the warmer climates of Italy and France; in northern Europe the overall effect in costume was one of voluminous folds rather than the light styles of the south. Nonetheless, European costume was, on the whole, more elegant than had been the fussy styles of the Romanesque period — clothing was increasingly tailored to the shape of the body and limbs and less effort expended on the addition of intricate details. For both men and women gowns were long, and, rarely, amongst the nobility at least, came above the knee; arms were never exposed for this would have been a sign of immodesty; if a wide-sleeved garment was worn, the arm was always covered with the tight-fitting sleeve of an undershirt. Despite this, women's clothing was invariably cut in pleasing, if not seductive, ways, and it was during the thirteenth century that the habit of swinging the hips when walking was developed. In order to achieve an attractive look, material was always cut on the cross, (diagonally to the grain of the cloth), allowing it to hang naturally in graceful folds around the contours of the figure.

The cut of clothing tended to follow classical lines in the thirteenth century, particularly in Italy, where long gowns would be gathered up into one or more bands to facilitate

11

movement. Men's clothes were more practical especially during the reigns of Henry III and Edward I who set personal examples of simplicity. This was certainly so for the working classes. Towards the end of the century a more voluptuous flowing look developed, presaging the heavy drapes and folds of the period to follow.

A wide range of materials was available to the tailor — woollen cloths (both domestically woven and, in the case of more exotic types, imported from the Middle East), linens ranging from fine lawn to heavy canvas, and cotton in a variety of weights. In addition to these, a number of more exotic materials was also available. Italian velvet was widely used to obtain a rich effect, and from Spain, Sicily and Venice came silks, heavy or light, in many different finishes, including gold and silver, to give a rich luxurious look for both secular and clerical garb. The delicate, transparent veils, so popular from this time onwards, were frequently made from fine silk.

Linings and trimmings of fur were standard for the nobility who alone were permitted to wear ermine and sable. Squirrel, badger, lamb, fox and even rabbit adorned the gowns of those not so highly-born.

Thirteenth and fourteenth century taste favoured bright colours in gem-stone shades and striking patterns. Bold colours dominated courtly gatherings and the parti-coloured or striped look was particularly fashionable. The common people, however, had to settle for the more sober hues, which could be made easily at home from natural dyes. Blue, grey, brown, red, orange, violet and green were all popular.

Plain colours were standard for many garments, or alternatively, designs were applied to the fabric. These consisted of all-over patterns developed from geometrical shapes or natural images — birds or leaves for example.

Amongst the inferior orders plaids and stripes were likely to have been standard patterns, although stripes, especially horizontal ones, were adopted by all strata of society. Within the stripes small repeated motifs sometimes figured — fleurs de lis, diamonds, ovals, crosses, trefoils, etc. Patterns might also be restricted to borders only — hemlines, necks, buttonbands and cuffs. The crusaders' habit of wearing a large cross motif emblazoned on their tunic fronts led in time to the wearing of heraldic emblems by civilians as well. Worn by men and women, such devices would extend from neck to hip, sometimes lower for women.

Courtiers and noblemen would decorate some costumes with jewels and precious stones at the throat or hem, fixing them in gold mesh or even solid silver and gold settings, but the difficulty of wearing clothes burdened with this extra weight restricted the style to the more ceremonial occasions. Jewels might also ornament the sleeves, belts, shoes and scabbards of the upper classes.

By the end of this period, the decay of feudalism was well under way, and the growing affluence of the middle-classes brought to the whole country an increase in trade and wealth, which was reflected in later periods in costumes more sumptuous than ever.

Men's costume   The basic garment worn by all men was the chemise. This was a loose shirt which might extend in length from mid-thigh to calf, and it was slit at both the front and the back. The neckline was a simple round cut with a short slit at the throat. For the peasant classes, the shorter chemise was often the only over-garment worn and it is most useful to the theatrical costumier in this context. In order to maximise free movement the tails could be tucked up into the belt.

Men of *higher classes* wore a variety of outer coverings over the chemise, and it is these outer clothes which characterise most clearly the costume of the period. The cote was a long skirted tunic which fell to below the knee or even to the ankle, with sleeves and body cut in one piece, giving a loose flowing effect to the garment as a whole. A wide neckline below the collar-bone was typical of the cote, and sleeves were narrow and close-fitting, buttoning on the outside from the elbow to a tight cuff. It was belted above the hips and any fullness in the body hung a little over the belt. Chemise and cote fitted close to the figure and might be worn without any other covering, at least for indoor use.

It was, however, usual to wear other garments over the cote, particularly outdoors, and the most usual of these outer covers was the surcote, probably the commonest outer garment to be seen at this time. It was a sleeveless tunic, looser and wider than the cote, and it fell to knee or ankle length, sometimes belted; the shorter varieties were often spot-patterned. Like the chemise it was slit in the back and occasionally the front, with the tails tucked into the belt if it was necessary for the feet to be free. The

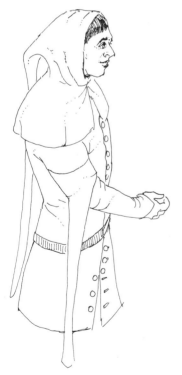

Cote-hardie with tippets on the sleeves. A liripipe is also worn

14

neckline was slit at the throat to admit the head and was similar to that of the cote or might be turned back to give the appearance of lappets. Some surcotes had a hood attached to the neckline, and slits at hip level (fitchets) in order to give access to a purse attached to a belt beneath. Another version of the surcote had sleeves, which were half-or full-length and necessarily bulky enough to accommodate the sleeves of the cote, although occasionally they would be buttoned down to the wrist like those of the cote. Surcote sleeves took a variety of styles, varying from very short cap-sleeves to full-length sleeves, which were often left unfastened to fall loose from the elbow, revealing the sleeves of the cote beneath. The surcote was belted or unbelted indiscriminately.

The three garments, chemise, cote and surcote make a good basic costume for a man of the period and in themselves they offer considerable scope for a variety of styles and effects. There were, however, other garments which can usefully be used to give an authentic range of costumes for stage use.

After 1300, clothes tended to become more close-fitting, following the lines of the body, with less fullness in the skirts. An example of this is the cote-hardie, tight-waisted, with a single skirt attached. The sleeves were short and often worn with tippets — long pieces of material hanging down from the elbow. The cote-hardie was a knee-length garment and had a shallow, wide neckline lower than that of the cote. Invariably the cote-hardie was worn in conjunction with the chaperon, a hooded shoulder cape extending from the neck to the upper chest and arms. Body and skirt were joined and the seam covered with a belt.

Between the chemise and the outer garment a man might wear a fur-lined or quilted doublet, known as a gipon, a waist length (or to the knees) jacket, sleeved or un-sleeved, intended to give extra warmth. At this time, the gipon was always worn under the cote-hardie, and is only of interest because its padding accentuated the narrow-waist look of the cote-hardie and because when the cote-hardie sleeves were short, its own tight sleeves (if any) showed from elbow to wrist. During the Renaissance, when the term 'doublet' came into general use for the gipon it became a more prominent item of clothing.

Another version of the sleeved surcote was called a garde-corps or hery-goud, a voluminous garment which fell in

The man is wearing a heri-goud,
a voluminous over-tunic c 1272

folds to the knees or ankles and had very wide sleeves extending well beyond the hands. In order to allow the hands to reach out, the sleeve had a long vertical slit cut about elbow level; the rest of the sleeve from elbow to wrist would then hang loose below the arm. The hery-goud was basically a substantial over-tunic, hooded and worn without a belt; it was particularly popular in Italy, where it was worn in many different styles, usually with side slits.

The tabard style over-garment was also occasionally seen; it was worn perhaps over a chemise or a cote. The sides of this garment were slit to the armpit and then fastened at waist level. The tabard had also a front slit to facilitate riding.

The usual *undergarments* for men of all classes were simple close-fitting drawers which were hidden by the chemise or cote, but might be glimpsed if the skirts of the over-garment were tucked up into the belt. Braies, a type of knee or ankle length bulky hose, rather like breeches, were worn by the lower classes. Worn long they might be gartered at the knee, or, in the case of shorter versions might be knotted above the knee, the calves left bare.

Men of the nobility would wear well-fitting *hose* beneath their tunics, and in the case of the shorter styles this was essential. Such hose was made as seamed stockings, separate for each leg, and in many cases covered the foot as well as the leg. It was attached with straps or brooches to the belt of the underwear. Alternatively, the hose might be fitted with a strap beneath the foot. Elastic cloth, wool, or more rarely silk were all used for hose which may occasionally even have been knitted, although there is some doubt about the prevalence of knitting as a craft in Europe before the seventeenth century. Gradually the popularity of long hose led to a shortening of the under-drawers to which it was attached. One piece hose was, however, not unknown at this time, being worn in France with a parti-coloured pattern, but this style was not general throughout Europe until later. If the cote was hitched up for some outdoor activity such as hawking, the hose tops, often embroidered, could be seen.

Hose was not always full-length and might be worn to knee or thigh level only, perhaps held with a garter; shorter varieties were particularly adopted by the lower classes. Parti-colouring was a popular decoration for hose, worn often with matching tunics; patterns of small designs or spots were also common.

Long pointed shoe c 1307

Long pointed shoe c 1315

Ankle high pointed shoe c 1315

Peasants might dispense with hose as such, and wear only short boots to protect their feet.

Footwear   During this period (as indeed through all periods throughout history) *shoes* were extremely varied and a large number of different styles can be found. These are based upon a few types only which we shall consider here.

Peasants frequently went barefoot about their work or wore only cloth ankle bindings to guard against scratches and cuts. Alternatively they wore close-fitting, heavy calf-length boots. These short boots were very popular with all classes, and ranged from the ordinary man's simple leather boots to the refined fur-lined styles of the wealthy. These latter would be made from very soft, flexible leather slit up to the instep and fastened with buttons, or made as simple slip-on shoes. In order to keep the wearer above the mud and wet such boots were worn with wooden pattens, which were simply thick slip-on soles.

As an alternative to a pair of shoes protection for the foot might consist only of leather soles attached to the hose.

Shoe shapes followed the outline of the foot in the main, although toe points were the subject of much attention, often extending several inches (and occasionally more) beyond the actual end of the foot. Long toe points were very much favoured as a fashion for all styles of shoe, from ankle-height slippers to thigh boots and are perhaps, more than any other feature, typically associated with this period and the next. The shorter shoes, below or above the ankle, were worn generally by all classes, but tall boots were not so common, usually being used for riding and necessarily restricted to those classes which could afford them.

Amongst the *higher classes*, shoe decoration was elaborate and involved the addition of embroidery, jewellery and expensive linings (often fur) to the shoes. Various types of tracery and cut-outs might be found in all types of shorter footwear.

The normal *outer covering* was the mantle or cape, a long circular or semi-circular garment slit entirely up the front and fastened on the right shoulder or at the throat. Alternatively, the cape was of the tabard style already mentioned, but completely slit up the sides with an opening at the neck for the head. Very long capes were usually worn for formal

17

Cardinals hat c 1528

Flat type of bonnet with feather
c 1547

Liripipe hat c 1299

or ceremonial occasions, indoors as well as out; for travelling the cape did not reach the ground. A shorter cape with a hood was often worn to combat wet and cold, this being a version of the chaperon, already mentioned; it was particularly favoured in France. A variety of hoods were worn, either with or without a cape or cloak. Popular styles were the capucheron — a simple folded rectangular hood or the chaperon style of hood and shoulder cover all in one.

Headdress   Many different kinds of hat were worn during this period. Caps were fairly small and unpretentious, covering the crown of the head, and having the appearance of a stiff beret, usually with a short tail on top. Felt, cotton, wool, fur and beaver were favourite materials. Some caps had ear flaps at the sides, sometimes extending to a complete bonnet which reached over the sides of the head and down to the neck. This latter style was usually of linen or silk, white or black, fastening under the chin, and was popular throughout the period, being known as a coif. It was worn by men of all classes, either alone or, frequently, with a small cap on top and may be used as a typical thirteenth and fourteenth century head-dress. The coif might be embroidered with motifs or decorated with geometrical designs. Contrasting segments of material were also used as an alternative to the plain coif.

During the earlier years of the thirteenth century the Phrygian cap style was still to be seen. Such hats resembled that traditionally associated with Punch — an upturned cone with the point curving slightly forward.

For travelling, the usual hat was a large, low-crowned hat with a broad brim which might be worn with a string under the chin to enable it to be pushed back off the head. The brim was sometimes turned up, either in the front or the back.

The hood alone, or as part of a cloak, remained the popular head covering, but in the latter part of this period, it developed from a simple loose head covering to include a long 'liripipe' or tail piece which stemmed from the point at the top and eventually became perhaps 60 or 90 cm (2 or 3 ft) long, sometimes stuffed to give it stiffness and shape. This tailpiece might hang forward or backwards and occasionally it was stiffened to such a degree that it stuck out horizontally.

Country people invariably wore coarsely made straw hats which resembled the broad-brimmed travelling hats.

Man in a gipon with hip belt, hose and calf length boots. A mantle attached from the shoulder

The soldier on the right is wearing the hauberk with a coif of mail protecting the head, over this is worn a leather jerkin, on his head he is wearing a helmet known as the kettle-hat. The hose is bound by cross-gartering. The soldier on the left is wearing a similar uniform with the exception of a coarse woollen hood and mantle (c 1315)

Rushes or even tree bark were used to make these hats.

Royal crowns were of simple, low style, without elaborate decoration.

The length of *men's hair* was usually not extravagant — cut in a bob at the sides at the level of the jaw and with a long curl across the forehead. Present day collar-length styles make it fairly easy to simulate this. At the back the hair fell to the nape of the neck and was usually waved or curled either in a single scroll curl or in ringlets. This was a uniform style throughout the period, although some wore a centre parting or a straightforward fringe. Most men (particularly the young) were clean shaven. The few beards seen were normally short and sometimes double-pointed. Clipped moustaches (if any) are also typical of the period, and more rarely a beard of 7 or 10 cm (3 or 4 in.) would be worn by an older man.

Ecclesiastical costume The vestments of an English bishop consisted of the mitre, chasuble and for parliamentary occasions, the alb and cope; these are illustrated. Other clergy, from priests to cardinals, wore a characteristic broad-brimmed hat; the number of tassels on the string indicated the rank of the wearer — a priest wore one, a bishop three, and a cardinal seven.

Monastic orders wore the normal civilian costume, gown or cote (usually girded) and hood, but in sombre, plain colours. The particular orders differed only in the colours worn, usually either brown or white.

Women's clothes resembled men's in many ways, although they were generally longer than comparative masculine styles. As with men, the basic feminine garment was the chemise, a long, high necked undershirt reading down to the instep with long, close-fitting sleeves. This was often the only indoor wear of the lower classes. Over this chemise, a variety of gowns would be worn. The most usual was the cote or kirtle, a loose fitting gown with long sleeves which were either loose, cut in one with the body, or tight, occasionally laced. The fullness of the body was gathered at the waist, and it was belted above the hips, the long tongue of the belt trailing down to the knees. The neck of the cote was slit a little down the front and then fastened with a brooch or lacing. Alternatively, a short U-neck opening might be worn. The front might have fitchets (pocket slits) giving

access to the purse worn underneath. A woman's rank would dictate the quality of material used for her cote. The simple cote and chemise is the typical dress of peasant women of the time. Together with a straw hat they comprise a classic peasant outfit, although they would, in this case be shorter, or tucked up into the girdle for ease of movement.

Women also wore the surcote over the cote; a long garment with voluminous folds and a wide back, the surcote was worn in many styles and was generally closer-fitting at the waist and hips than that worn by men. Variations were both sleeved and sleeveless. In the early part of the period the sleeves were wide and capacious, but later they became tight-fitting, buttoned sleeves which were, as with the masculine styles, left open to fall from the elbow. The armholes of this latter style were fairly snug-fitting. A combination of these styles, wide to the elbow and tight thereafter was also worn. Side slits were sometimes incorporated in the skirt, and were left unfastened part way up. The surcote was most often unbelted and, like the cote, had fitchets or pockets in front and at hip level. With the sleeveless surcote, the armholes sometimes became long slits themselves, showing a contrasting cote beneath. This practice was widespread amongst women who were anxious to impress one another with their finery and it is a classic feature of this period and the next, indeed, an essential point to remember when costuming women is the importance of the combined effect of garments such as the cote and surcote when made in contrasting colours, as they usually were. The patches of undergarment showing at neck, sides, hem and cuffs might be almost as important to a woman as the overgown. The neck opening of the surcote was wide, extending onto both shoulders. Another particularly Italian style was a knee length surcote with a deep jagged hem which contrasted well with a long cote worn underneath. Styles in other European countries were less individual.

Women in the *higher classes* sometimes chose to wear a very plain, unbelted gown, instead of the surcote; this relied for its effect on flowing folds of rich material, set off with a single brooch fastening at the neck.

In France women wore the garde-corps which, like the male equivalent, had long wide sleeves with an arm-slit at elbow height. Equipped with a hood, the garde-corps was usually rather longer and more voluminous than the man's version, extending right to the ground. As a rule, French

Lady in a cote-hardie with a row of buttons down the front, long sleeved to the wrist, with tippets, vertical slits called fitchets are in the front of the cote-hardie. The plaits in the hair covered in gold or silver tubes on either side of the face, a veil and fillet is worn. The man on the right wearing a long cote-hardie with a short shoulder cape. He wears the tall round hat (c 1360).

23

women enjoyed clothes which were more carefully tailored to the shape of the body than in the North. In the warmer climate of Italy classical style gowns were popular — these often had split sleeves and shoulders which were held together with spaced ties. The skirts were very long and often gathered up to facilitate movement.

For *outdoor wear* and protection against the weather women wore a cloak or mantle. The mantle was a long, full, circular or semicircular garment which was worn with or without a hood and was fastened at the neck with a clasp, brooch or cord. Generally women's capes followed the same lines as men's and were worn indoors at court and for ceremonies, outdoors for travelling. The ceremonial cape is, for both sexes, an especially impressive garment when used appropriately in a play or pageant. Women of the nobility had decoratively lined cloaks and capes which might even be used as dressing-gowns. Fur trimmings at collar and hem were, of course, always favoured.

Women's hose was the same as men's during this period, knitted or made from seamed cloth — linen or silk — and held up with garters which might have a buckle attached. Hose was, however, rarely seen because of the ubiquitous use of long gowns.

Women's shoes were also similar to men's but did not come above the ankle and lacked the turned-down cuff-like tops of some men's styles. The short ankle length shoes, sumptuously decorated for the upper classes, would be fastened with laces or buttons, or were just simple slip-on shoes. As with hose, it should be noted, long gowns tend to make women's shoes less noticeable than men's.

Women's hair was the subject of more attention than men's and was symbolically much more important. Long loose hair with no head-dress of any kind was the custom for queens and unmarried girls, but was considered improper for married women.

During the thirteenth century the hair was parted in the centre and tied either into a bun on the nape of the neck or in a chignon hanging down to the shoulders. Alternatively, it would be fastened up, leaving the neck bare. Thus tied back the hair was encased in a linen bag or a fine net-

General characteristics of the early Gothic period are shown by the lady on the left, c 1270. She is carrying a spindle and thread, a very useful hand property. The lady on the right is wearing a costume of c 1350. Settings are suggested by stone arches and doorways

The exaggerated male silhouette of the late Gothic period shows the extreme fashion compared with the simplicity of the female costume. Dagged or scalloped clothes and dangling bells were very popular

Lady of the Royal family
wearing a surcote with close
sleeves heavily draped mantle
of silk. She is wearing the
wimple, veil and fillet and
crown. The young boy is dressed
in a simple knee-length tunic
with a buttoned gipon sleeve
showing (c 1290)

work of gold mesh which might be set with gems. This was known as a crespin or crispine. The net was attached to a metal fillet around the brow. A strip of linen or transparent cloth, 5 to 7 cm (2 - 6 in.) wide (a barbier or barbette) was then passed under the chin and round onto the top of the head, being tied there or at the side. In another style it was worn from one side of the head under the chin to the other, fastened to hair braided over the ears. A small cap or stiff linen circlet fitted over the barbette, or alternatively a second strip of cloth would be tied around the top of the head.

Later on in the century the fashion was to tie the hair into buns on either side of the head, over the ears; this superceded the earlier style by 1300. The barbette and head band style was, at the end of the period, dropped in favour of a band or circlet worn like a crown and shaped oval to fit over the buns at the sides of the head. This circlet or fillet, splayed out slightly in the manner of a crown, was of stiff linen at first, but came to be frilled, scalloped or goffered later in the period. In the case of older women it was often studded with jewels and richly decorated. It would be worn with or without a linen skull-cap beneath. In time the fillet was completely covered over to produce the women's coif, or pill-box style hat, worn frequently over the barbette and crispine. Royal or noble personage would wear the crown on top of or around the coif.

A *classic headdress* for women of this period, particularly older or religious women and widows was the gorget or wimple. This was a strip of cloth fastened around the neck and up the sides of the head, pinned at the back. This sometimes extended high up the head, leaving only the hair at the crown of the head visible. More commonly it was worn with a head veil which hung down the back of the head and was held in place with a circlet.

Various other hats were worn either alone or in conjunction with these items and after 1300 women increasingly wore the same styles as men — the coif, or bonnet, and the chaperon, with or without a large-brimmed hat which might also be worn alone.

Children's costumes present no special difficulty for the costumier, for older children wore simple versions of their parents clothes, the cote and surcote, although those from

The Jewish merchant on the left wearing long cote-hardie with mantle fastened on the right shoulder with decorated ankle shoes, is wearing the tall pointed hat peculiar to Jewish costume of the thirteenth century. The young lady on the right with surcote and kirtle sleeves to the waist, being unmarried her hair hangs loosely down

the nobility might be turned out very smartly. Young girls wore their hair free and did not cover it. Infants were always swaddled with bands of cloth which might sometimes have been embroidered.

Accessories   Ornamentation was a subject which occupied the minds of all at the time. Women had a good deal of time in which to embroider clothing, and it was customary amongst those who could afford it to wear very elaborately decorated garments.

Brimmed hats could be trimmed with gold and silver lace and jewelled with gems or semi-precious stones. The same kind of decoration, including gold mesh was applied to the gloves of the period, and, in the way of other jewellery, rings, bracelets and brooches were favourites, although necklaces and earrings were rarely seen. Brooches were used on capes, neck openings, hats and might depict the wearers own insignia. Purses were worn by everyone, usually attached to the belt of the cote or surcote, and it was the custom amongst some people to wear a dagger slipped through the purse.

The general impression to convey is one of expensive garments, richly decorated for formal occasions, but less extravagance for everyday life away from court.

Late Gothic 1350-1450

The Late Gothic period was a time of increasing freedom, both social and economic, for European peoples now being liberated from the constraints of feudal society. Aristrocratic influence was declining and a new, prosperous middle class, growing wealthy on the proceeds of international trade, was challenging the supremacy of the old order. The importance of commerce and the rise of urban centres are strong forces from this period on — the general increase in the wealth of all European countries made possible a flourishing culture which placed more emphasis on variety and individualism and less on the generalised extremes of the old feudal classes.

As well as the overland trade routes through Europe, the sea route from the Mediterranean via the Atlantic to the North Sea was more extensively used, effectively linking

Group in ecclesiastical clothes
of the period

the cultures of North and South, and making possible a great increase in the volume of trade.

Ecclesiastical influence too was being slowly eroded — the new philosophy of humanism took a firm hold in the academic world and there was a marked trend towards individualism as the bourgeouisie, enjoying the fruits of their new-found wealth, strove to imitate a nobility which was determined to preserve its superiority.

The leaders of fashion throughout Europe were the courts, particularly those in France, Spain and Italy, which had greater wealth than England or Germany; the French court influence, in particular, was pre-eminent throughout Europe. New ideas about fashion transformed the earlier attitudes towards clothes. The aesthetic sense was strong, leading people to think more carefully about the artistic effect of costume and the impression which could be made with carefully chosen combinations of style and materials. Increasingly, caprice, rather than function, became the deciding factor in the choice of clothing. The search was not simply for a pleasing effect, but for an ideal beauty to which all women aspired.

The loose garments of the Early Gothic period gave way at this time to the stiffer look of the doublet and the pleated, fitted garments of both men and women. The prevailing look was generally shorter for men (with the notable exception of the houppelande) and for both sexes tailored in a more sophisticated way.

Extravagance was a key feature of the period for both sexes. The wealthier classes could afford to indulge their taste for luxury and spend freely on clothes, and were fond of quantities of superfluous material which trailed behind them on the ground. However, clothes were expensive, and extravagance which was not done deliberately for effect was less prevalent. Linings of fur and rich fabrics lent emphasis to the impression of gratuitous excess which is perhaps more strikingly displayed by the extraordinary styles of women's headdresses which were purely decorative as they kept the hair in place.

Women's necklines plunged to extremes, producing decolletages which reached to the waist in some cases, showing the cote beneath. Shoe length, too, was often excessive, ostensibly because the flapping effect of a long toe was popular.

As the European textile industry became more advanced

A lesson in warfare, soldier in short tunic and liripipe hood. The young boy on the right is wearing a sleeveless embroidered jerkin with long full sleeves

an increasing range of materials was available to the manufacturers of these sumptuous clothes. Technical advances in dying and weaving brought linens, cottons, silks and woollens within the pockets of many more people than before and new materials such as taffeta and velvet were produced. Cloth might be obtained plain or patterned — flowers, foliage and geometric designs were still popular, and they would appear either as small motifs, including monograms and insignia, all over the fabric, or in large repeated designs. The fashion for stripes was retained in this period, as was the taste for the parti-coloured look which was as popular as ever. This might be simple balancing of blocks of colour, or it might involve a counter-change effect using the pattern of the material. Heraldic devices, large and small persisted.

In general there was, during the Late Gothic period, much more attention to detail, reflecting the insistence on individual styles and new ideas. The decoration of clothes was characterised by the universal mania amongst men, and less frequently, women, for dagged edges, cut or slashed to give a regular or random jagged look. These edges would be trimmed in bright colours to contrast with the main colour of the garment. In the fifteenth century borders were, for both sexes, more characteristically fur-trimmed. Ermines and squirrel were favourites amongst those who could afford them, sheep, lamb and even rabbit or fox for the less pretentious.

The preponderance of jewellery which marked out the wealthiest members of the nobility in the Early Gothic period was still a powerful feature in this. Some men would wear about their necks the ornamental chain of a chivalric organisation if they belonged to one, this resembling the chain worn by present-day mayors. Women had, by now, begun to wear necklaces and pendants, and rings and brooches were standard wear for all wealthy people. As the art of fine metalwork improved so did the settings for gems and the hilts of swords and daggers.

The spirit of the Late Gothic era was noticeably one of change and experiment, the burgeoning of an interest in material prosperity and secular art which was to flourish during the Renaissance. When costuming the period remember that men and women of the nobility strove to assert their individuality and to maintain standards of dress which would emphasise their supremacy. The peasant classes would

The figure on the left in a cote-hardie over a padded gipon cut short with the neck and the sleeves of the houppelande, the sleeves are known as the bagpipe sleeves. Coloured hose were popular. Tall round crowned hat. The figure on the right is wearing an open houppelande which is long to the ankle, turned-up trilby-type hat. The daggers were carried hanging in the centre at the waist (c 1400)

be dressed in much the same way as they had been previously. Their sober garments were short, practical and unfussy. Between these two extremes, the merchants and traders endeavoured to establish for themselves a more comfortable standard of living, in emulation of the elegant life-styles of their betters.

Men's costume   The chemise remained the basic garment, long-sleeved and thigh length, and over this was worn a short jacket, the doublet (the French pourpoint), which had grown out of the style for such garments which had first occurred in the previous period. The doublet was normally sleeved and fastened up either the front or the back. Occasionally it would be sleeveless, and worn under a second doublet to give extra warmth. When worn as the outer covering, the doublet was tailored closely to the body and padded or quilted. A straight skirt, often no more than hip length was attached to the doublet at the waist. In France this garment was known as a pourpoint, well padded at the breast, sides and hips and very close-fitting in order to emphasise the slim waist. Buttons or lacing fastened the pourpoint up the front. The sleeves, which were characteristically padded at the shoulders, took any of the many styles seen on other garments.

The pourpoint or doublet would either be worn along or with a thigh length gown like the cote-hardie. Sometimes pleated, this gown was belted at the waist and generally had full sleeves in order to accommodate the padded sleeves of the pourpoint.

The overall effect of the doublet is one of an accentuated body outline — broad chests and tight waist — which contrasts completely with the loose untailored styles of Early Gothic costume. The principal long gown of this period, the houppelande, was also cut in a much more sophisticated way than had been previous garments — it too was a typical costume for men who were now much more attentive to fashion as a means of embellishing the human form.

Major changes were made in the styles for large gowns, although amongst older men and peasants the traditional cote-hardie and cote were still prevalent. The surcote had, for men, by now almost died out, although it was occasionally still seen. More fashionable men adapted the cote-hardie to create a shorter, thigh-length tunic, with a round neck and fastening from neck to hem with buttons. The sleeves were tight fitting, with the characteristic buttons from

Lady in the butterfly headdress supported by wire made of white lawn. Gorget around the neck. Open sleeved cote-hardie with sleeves of undergown showing. Man on the right wearing the short houppelande and the long dagged hanging sleeves (early fifteenth century)

elbow to wrist, and the garment was worn with a heavily ornamented hip belt. Sleeve shapes changed towards the end of the fourteenth century and contrast-lined tippets hanging from an elbow-length sleeve might be worn. Alternatively, a baggy sleeve, fitting close at armhole and cuff was popular; it might have an elbow-height slit to allow the arm to reach out easily. Sometimes, mainly in Germany, such a sleeve would have no cuff opening at all, thus resembling a balloon hanging from the shoulder with a slit for the arm.

A plain, long, unbelted gown was occasionally worn by men of higher rank, particularly in Italy and amongst scholars and other less extravagant folk. This garment was unwaisted, falling to ankle length, with capacious but not excessive sleeves.

The most characteristic garment of this period was the houppelande, a flowing, floor-length gown which was made in a variety of styles and much decorated. The houppelande was occasionally knee-length, but more usually it draped on the floor and might be slit up to thigh level to ease walking. The houppelande was cut closely, but not tightly, to the shoulder and body, and it fell in graceful, even folds (which may have been fastened in place) from the waist, where it was held with a belt, to the floor. It was made from four pieces of material, seamed at front, back and sides. In the fifteenth century the houppelande was frequently fastened from the neck to the hem with buttons or hooks and eyes concealed in a front fold. The sleeves were usually large and open, and might have large trailing cuffs which hung well down towards or even onto the floor. This style of sleeve was also adopted by some fashionable young men who wore it with a tight doublet. The dagged look was often a feature of the houppelande — any edge or hem might be decorated in this way. Other sleeve styles included a tight sleeve (as had the doublet) which in some cases flared a little at the wrist like a ruff, and also a sleeve which was close-fitting from cuff to elbow, and then bagged out up to the arm-hole, possibly decorated with slashes to show a contrasting lining.

A particular characteristic of the houppelande was a high collar which occasionally extended as far as the back of the head and was fastened at the front. More often it reached to the nape of the neck and was cut with a V-shaped opening at the throat, or alternatively was buttoned up to the chin. This collar also appeared with the doublet, and was a typical

The houppelande worn by the
man on the right is worn just
above knee-length, the sleeve
being full and gathered at the
shoulder. The collar of the gipon
shows above the neck of the
houppelande. The shoes are
very pointed and worn with
pattens. He is wearing the
chaperon. The page on the right
is wearing the short Italian
style tunic with small round
hat

feature of a man of fashion at this time. Alternative collars on the houppelande included a flat turned-down collar or a shorter upright collar which allowed a tall doublet collar to show underneath. The houppelande was, occasionally, worn without a collar.

Men's hose became longer during this period reaching right up to the crotch. At first they were in the form of long stockings, attached with laces or points to the doublet or the underdrawers, which, by now, with the advent of shorter garments had become mere trunks. In the case of very short-skirted doublets, hose was made in one with a cod-piece, resembling modern tights. As previously it was close-fitting with seams, or even knitted in some cases, and the advent of the hip-length garments gave much more prominence to hose and to the way it was made and fastened. At the foot the various fittings — full foot, stirrup strap, leather sole etc. were all popular. Materials used for making hose have been described in the Early Gothic section.

Among the *peasants*, cross-gartered breeches were still traditional, or cloth gaiters might be used to protect the shins. If wearing full hose peasants usually rolled them down to the knee, to facilitate bending for manual work. In summer, they would dispense with hose altogether.

Footwear   The long-toed *shoe* which became popular in the last period increased in length until by the end of the fourteenth century it was in some cases attached to the knee with a thin chain. By the end of this period, however, the style had waned and shoes became a more normal length once again. Long boots for riding were still standard wear; otherwise outdoor wear comprised the shorter calf-length boot, made from soft leather for the gentry and more crudely constructed for peasants. Boots might be laced up one or other side, or buckled at the side or the instep. Short ankle length shoes were still much worn indoors and varied from simple slip-on types to highly decorated laced or buttoned shoes. Outdoors, they would be worn with pattens. Whilst the long toe point was in vogue, the shape of the patten conformed also to this style. European peasants often wore a simple wooden clog or sabot of traditional style.

Men's hairstyles remained much the same as they had been over the previous century, usually curled or bobbed to jaw length (sometimes straight) and cut with a curl along the

The gentleman on the left is wearing the short houppelande with fur-trimmed hanging sleeves. The gentleman on the right is wearing heavily draped mantle. The head is covered with the chaperon or converted hood (early fifteenth century)

forehead. Beards became increasingly popular, and were much the same as they had been in the past — short-clipped and single- or double-pointed with short moustaches. Longer beards were, again, usually worn by older men. At the end of the period a vogue for shorter cropped hair came in, occasionally shaved in a short pudding-basin style.

Headdress The sorts of hats available were numerous and included all those previously worn, particularly the coif, which was as popular as ever. Brimmed hats, worn with or without the coif, often had a higher crown than before, sometimes a very high bell-crown. The wide-brimmed travelling hat of straw or felt was still widely used.

Innovations at this time included a small high-crowned hat with no brim, presumably wired into shape, and, particularly characteristic of this period, a new method of donning the chaperon, or shoulder length hood. Instead of being worn over the neck and shoulders, the opening framing the face, the chaperon was placed onto the crown of the head, its bulk hanging in folds to one side, and the tail, now often extremely long, either hanging loose at the side or wound round the head or shoulders. It was soon found easier to sew the chaperon into this shape, or to make it up from separate pieces of material. Towards the end of the period this style evolved into a hat with a padded brim and skull-cap, with the hanging folds and tail-piece sewn on as extras. This was a roundel, a stiffer, more formal hat than the chaperon.

The *royal crown* was taller and a little more ornate than in the earlier times, but the simple crown was still retained by the nobility.

Women's costume. The chemise was still the normal under-garment for women, and was, in this period, because of the increasing popularity of décolleté neckline, often visible at the neck. Over this, women still wore the cote or the cote-hardie. The former was the same garment as had previously been worn, and was also, in a somewhat different version known as the corset. Generally speaking, the corset was laced at the front, whereas the cote was fastened (if at all) at the back. The corset might have short sleeves, like the old surcote, to show the chemise sleeves beneath. The front-laced corset was worn with overgowns by peasant women, but was otherwise worn as an overdress, except sometimes in Italy and Southern Europe.

The man on the left in knee-length houppelande with long and wide sleeves is wearing a chaperon hat. The gentleman on the right is wearing the Italian style parti-coloured hose with knee-length gown with velvet collar and slashed sleeves and a velvet cap

41

Sleeveless surcote worn with a crespine headdress c 1350

The cote-hardie, still worn by women, was tailored to the hips where it was belted, and then fell in long skirts to the ground. The body, wide-necked, was buttoned down to the waist and the sleeves fell in tippets from the elbow, as did the men's.

A style typical of the early and mid-fourteenth century, and one especially suitable for use on the stage is a simply cut gown, tailored to the figure down to the waist and then falling to ground level in a full skirt. The neckline for this varied from a wide round cut to a V-shape of varying depth, showing a contrasting cote beneath. Deep side slits from hem to hip also allowed the colour of the cote to show next to that of the gown. The development of this gown was a feature of the Renaissance.

Particularly fashionable at this time was a version of the sleeveless surcote, which was cut away at the sides to give large armholes from armpit to hip, leaving only a strip of fabric, usually fur trimmed, at front and back. The wide, open neckline gave the effect of shoulder straps and the bodice extended right down to a broad hip-band from which the full skirts fell. The front of the bodice was decorated with a row of buttons from neck to hips. The bodice of the surcote extended so far below the waist that the open sides exposed the hip-belt and contrasting colours of the cote or cote-hardie beneath.

In later styles the hip-band of the surcote frequently dipped in a U-shape over the abdomen. France and northern European countries exaggerated this style as much as possible the French favouring a very full skirt gathered into the hip-band. In Germany a slimmer look was more popular — the surcote fitted close to the body, and did not stand out from the hips as it did in France. As with all overdresses and gowns the skirts of the surcote were richly lined in order to create the maximum effect when gathered or held up for walking. For the poorer classes, the old-style surcote was still used.

Outer garments   By the end of the fourteenth century women had followed men in adopting the houppelande as a general overgarment. Worn over the cote the houppelande was either tailored and unbelted or girded to a high waistline and pleated down to a full skirt. Unlike men's houppelandes the feminine version was always long. Sleeve styles were the same as for the men — capacious wide funnels, long trailing or hanging sleeves, baggy sleeves gathered in at the shoulder and cuffs or more simply (and very popular) narrow, to the cuff. Necklines varied considerably for the women's houppelande — the high collar was considerably exaggerated and imitated either the men's tail, stand-up, V-throated collar or assumed a decanter mouth style, curled away from the head at ear level. Another style was the flat, turned-down collar more or less folded back from the neck, combining with the deep decolletage to reveal the bodice of the cote and possibly beneath that, the chemise. By the end of this period the houppelande had evolved into a simpler garment like the gown already mentioned. This was part of a general trend, for both men and women, towards less voluminous (although no less extravagant) styles.

Elderly women wore a sober, ungirded houppelande without the deep neckline. For both men and women the houppelande became a standard outer garment, particularly if lined with fur, and the cloak and mantles of former times were less frequently used in everyday life.

For ceremonial use circular mantles were worn almost off the shoulder, hanging in a train at the back and lined with fur. They were fastened at the neck with jewelled cords. For more common use, when travelling for example, a cloak or hooded cloak sufficed. A typical cloak buttoned in front at the throat and had a high collar to cover that of the houppelande.

Hair   During this period women began to pay much more attention to their hair and head-dress than formerly. A wide variety of hat styles was prevalent, involving very many variations on a few basic themes.

Long hair styles were still restricted to unmarried women, Italian women especially were in the habit of wearing loose hairstyles, crowned with a garland of flowers or a long plait. Over the flowing locks might still be worn a simple circlet or chaplet, but married women, who wore their hair up, increasingly used elaborate forms of head-dress. At the end of the fourteenth century, a square-faced look was achieved by braiding the hair in vertical ringlets at the front of the head and sometimes encasing these in metal ornamental tubes which hung from the temples. A simpler style of head-dress was the goffered veil which formed an arch over the forehead and fell to the shoulders. This might be made from several layers of material. The veil could be worn plain, or

Headdress with a square look, encased in vertical metal ornamental tubes c 1420

Front of headdress edged with ruffles and gathering c 1370

43

44

decorated with network and worn over a fillet which showed at the forehead. Hair nets were generally used with all head-dresses, and usually had delicately worked ornamentation.

In order to fasten the hair up under the head-dress women coiled and braided it up over the ears, often shaving the forehead to give the impression of a high brow. Eyebrow plucking became more popular, as did dying the hair with saffron.

Headdress   At the beginning of the fifteenth century head-dress styles developed along broader and fuller lines, becoming increasingly elaborate, this was the beginning of a vogue for the complicated and the ornate which reached its peak in later periods. These head-dresses are generally more characteristic of the fifteenth century than the fourteenth.

The hair at the temples was often enclosed in decorative casings knows as 'templers', worn above or over the ears. These would be worn with an ornamental fillet, and a veil behind. The larger versions of the templers were wider and necessitated a much more substantial version of the fillet to hold them in place, again, usually with a veil. Such a head-dress might be fitted with a wired veil protruding like horns to the front sides of the head.

An extension of the side pieces in an upward curve above the head gave a heart-shaped look for yet another style. In an exaggerated form this appeared as a U-shaped padded veil forming a high crown above the head. The templers developed in this instance into an integral part of the head-dress which sat as one unit above the ears, with the hair shaved up to its edge. On the continent, a turban shaped head-dress resembling the male roundel was popular; it was formed from a padded ring worn over a hair net, the hair braided into a bun at each temple.

Gorget and wimple were still the standard wear for pious women, although amongst other women, the gorget was sometimes worn alone. More commonplace hats were the chaperon (worn alone or with another hat) and the brimmed felt and straw hats of previous periods.

It is more important to get the basic shape of the head-dress correct than it is to be accurate in detail. The aim should be to imitate the main characteristics – width, height, shape and obvious accessories such as veils or hair nets. The myriad idiosyncrasies of individual styles were far too numerous to be useful to the costumier, unless for some

Gentleman wearing the short houppelande over which he wears a voluminous mantle. Soft brimmed hat. Lady wearing the high-waisted dress and hanging fur sleeves. She is wearing the French style hennin steeple-shaped headdress (c 1450)

reason absolute realism is essential.

Footwear   Women's shoes showed very little beneath the voluminous skirts of the cote-hardie or the houppelande, but they resembled men's, although without the exaggerated toe-points. Short ankle shoes, often highly decorated and fastened over the instep with hooks, buttons, buckles or laces were usual, as were the simple slip-on shoes.

Renaissance 1450-1550

The Renaissance saw the establishment of trade as a vital force in European economy. The pioneering merchants of earlier centuries had created a network of trade routes and industrial centres which supplied Europe with a wide variety of luxuries and materials from both Western and Eastern cultures. Now that it was firmly rooted in the structure of European society, the middle class could afford not only the finery of elegant costumes but beautiful houses and furnishings in which to show off their wealth.

This universal prosperity stimulated cultural activity throughout Europe; the invention of printing and the voyage of Columbus are but two of the more famous events of an age in which initiative and enterprise were the characteristics of success.

Much of the detailed information we have about the costume of the Renaissance is provided by the huge variety of pictorial evidence left by the artists of the time — Holbein, Breughel, Durer, da Vinci, Titian, Boticelli, and the many others whose paintings have moulded our ideas about Renaissance lifestyles. The paintings, accessible nowadays to anyone who cares to visit a library or gallery, are a primary source for the costumier, providing details, not only of clothing, but of settings, architecture and social customs.

Architectural styles reflected the change from the inflexibility of the feudal system to a new era in which the pursuit of excellence was the aim of every educated man. Late Gothic blended with Renaissance neo-classicism to produce fine examples of both ecclesiastical and secular buildings — Hampton Court in England, the French chateaux and the work of Palladio in Italy.

Costume was caught in a phase of transition from the long

Priest in ecclesiastical vestments of late fifteenth century and executioner of the later fifteenth century

47

The lady in a close-fitting bodice kirtle with the decolletage filled in by a high-necked chemise. The man is wearing the short gown from which the slashed sleeves of the full skirted doublet are show (early sixteenth century)

The early Renaissance costumes are shown here in the Italian style, much favoured by Shakespeare. Simple arch settings are ideal for plays of this period

The late Renaissance costumes are characterised in the men's square look with the wide shoulders, short gowns and square toed shoes. The women's fashion of the gable headdress was the chief characteristic of the period. Panelled walls were also a feature

voluminous styles of the Gothic ages to the square, sturdy Tudor look. Brief doublets and floor-sweeping gowns co-existed; a strong tide of individualism inspired excesses of competition in which any new extravagance was an asset. Ornament took the form of bold designs or the famous slashed look which was universally applied to the sixteenth century to any item of male apparel, and some female too. In its most exaggerated form it was a predominantly German characteristic, but it pervaded the whole of Europe in its less absurd forms. The over-garment would be patterned with cuts, short and long, through which the contrasting cloth of the lining was puckered.

Other forms of ornamentation abounded — ribbons, curls, pleats, feathers, false sleeves tied on to the shoulders showing the brightly-coloured sleeves beneath. Buttons, pearls and embroidery all contributed to an overall impression of sumptuous, expensive clothing. Jewellery also was important: brooches, chains, necklaces and rings were univerally favoured by the upper classes. Much of this must, of necessity, be dispensed with for dramatic works, but the assiduous attention to details, so typical of the period, should be suggested.

Increasing quantities of fine materials were exported from the East to Europe — cloth from China, Egypt, Persia, Cyprus and other exotic sources found its way into the wardrobes of the rich and an enormous variety of silks, satins, velvet and taffeta from Italy augmented the traditional linens and woollens of the north. The trade in furs, too, was impressive — ermine, squirrel and beaver, marten, fox, otter and many others were hunted in great numbers to line and edge the clothes of every class, although the commoners had to make do with lamb, sheep, wolf and goat.

National characteristics, previously subordinated to the general trends in European costume, were now reflected in variations of the basic styles. Fashion was still led by the French who were masters at the art of cutting and tailoring a garment to produce a stylish fit. In Spain, stiff tightly laced bodices and full skirts presaged Elizabethan styles in the courts of Europe, but extravagance was not a feature of Spanish or Italian dress. It was the Germans who adopted the most outrageous modes, in contrast to soberer tastes in England where a rich, formal look was favoured.

However, the high incidence of international travel helped to spread new styles rapidly throughout Europe, giving a

The costume of the mercenary
soldier (landknecht) with his
large two handed sword (early
sixteenth century)

general corpus of basic characteristics to all European costume. Rich materials, close-fitting bodices, full skirts and wide hips, loose capacious sleeves and simply designed shoes are universal features.

During the early part of the period *men's hair* was usually bobbed at a moderate length as it had been for the last 200 years, or cut in a bowl shape above ear level, but as the Renaissance gathered pace the hair lengthened, reaching down to the shoulders, or might be clipped short. Where the hair was not naturally waved or curled it could be left straight. Some cuts were bushy at the sides and a page-boy cut with fringe was also current. The popularity of beards grew with the sixteenth century — the clipped short beard or moustache was occasionally seen, although for the most part men went clean shaven.

The variety of *head-gear* for both men and women at this time was considerable, and few general styles only can be outlined here. At the beginning of the period there were many variations on the low-crowned hat with a brim which might be turned up or down. Hats such as these would be worn square on the head or tilted to one side. The coif, usually in white linen, also came in many styles, principally as a simple bonnet covering the crown of the head and the ears and as such was a simple style often used by the peasants. A velvet cap with ear flaps like the coif was typical of scholars and elderly gentlemen.

In Italy a high-crowned brimless hat somewhat resembling a tall fez was popular, and a similar style, the brimless sugar loaf or flower-pot shape, was found in England. A turban-like brim was often added to these hats giving them a rather Eastern look.

In sixteenth century Germany, the hat worn to the exclusion of nearly any other was the barett, a low-crowned hat with a broad brim slashed at the edges and decorated with ribbon or contrasting pieces of material. The barett might well be set off with a few large feathers.

Simpler people and *peasants* adopted the coif, as described above, or the ever-popular wide-brimmed straw or felt hats. Hooded capes were still worn by the peasants. The chaperon lasted in vogue until about 1480, but was often worn off the head with the tail hanging down the back, more for ornament than for use.

Male 'halo' type bonnet decorated with jewels and ostrich feather tips (first third of the sixteenth century)

Slashed brim bonnet with a low crown (beginning of sixteenth century)

51

Large flat hat with narrow turned up brim (beginning of sixteenth century)

Wide slouched bonnet with slashed brim (early sixteenth century)

The lady in the German fashion with a full pleated skirt is close-fitting slashed sleeves and wearing a koller (short jacket). The man is dressed with the slashed doublet sleeve emerging from the short gown sleeves. Large flat tam-o-shanter style hat

Men always wore a hat in the presence of their peers and their inferiors but never in the presence of the king, who himself invariably did. The royal crown retained its relatively simple style, although the ornamentation was increasingly elaborate.

Over the chemise men adopted a shorter style tunic known as a doublet, a waistcoat-like garment, skirtless and fastening normally in the back, occasionally in front. The doublet would be worn with a variety of necklines — flat and cut low at the collar-bone, level, or plunging U-shaped to the waist. Later in the period, a high doublet collar which protruded out from beneath a covering garment was introduced. This would be fastened, or not, at will, or perhaps turned back to form revers or lapels. The sleeves of the doublet were usually tied into the armholes with points and through the gaps the cloth of the chemise could be seen. Alternatively, body and sleeves could be cut in one. Sleeve styles included the straight close-fitting sleeve or the baggy wrinkled sleeve, pleated into a snug fit at the wrist, especially if no jerkin was to be worn over the doublet. Large shoulder sleeves, wide down to the elbow and slim thereafter were also known. The front and sleeves of the doublet might be slashed to show the chemise cloth or a contrasting lining which was puckered through the slits. The essential feature of the doublet was the narrow waist and close fit which accentuated the broad shoulder of the wearer. It is this look which established itself in the predominant style of men's clothing during the Renaissance.

Over the doublet men wore the jerkin open at the front in order to show the doublet. If not worn open, the jerkin would be girded with a belt, cord or sash. The skirt of the jerkin extended to hip or, more often, knee-level, and the neck line varied from high collars with wide revers to low necks, square or round; the long decolletage, if any, was V- or U-shaped. In the early part of the period this was a shortened version of the cote-hardie, with a padded chest and shoulders and a short pleated skirt sitting high on the hips. Pleated centre panels extended above and below the waistline.

The old-style hanging sleeve with a vertical arm-slit at the elbow was adapted to the jerkin but there were many variations. Sleeves of the jerkin were naturally rather large and bulky in order to accomodate those of the doublet;

Flat cap with narrow straight brim (early sixteenth century)

Large slouched bonnet with wide brim over the forehead (early sixteenth century)

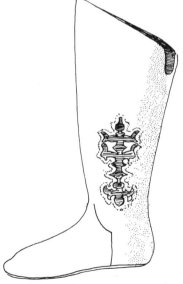

High boot (late fifteenth century)

they might be only short, to elbow length, very padded, or alternatively they would extend right down to the wrist, again puffed out considerably.

An innovation was the epaulet style cap sleeve, which hid the seam of the doublet armhole. In southern Europe, the doublet often had attached to it knee-length full skirts which stood out from the legs in a rather unusual style.

Peasants adopted a simple attire comprising the old-style long chemise with a tunic or jerkin. The chemise would be slit up the front to allow freedom of movement. The tunic was sleeveless or moderately full down to a tight cuff.

Over these basic jackets men wore a loose gown, both indoors and outdoors, although the undergarment would not necessarily include both jerkin and doublet. One or other only of these might be worn. The traditional long style was still worn, mainly by elder statesmen or scholars, but increasingly the fashion was for a thigh- or knee-length gown worn open in the front and pleated up into a short yoke at the front and the back. The open front would reveal the jerkin or doublet beneath, but it might sometimes be belted at the waist. The longer style of gown had a round neck with the jerkin or doublet collar protruding up from beneath. Belted or loose, it was pleated both back and front and slit to the knee. The gown was sometimes sleeveless with wide, bordered armholes trimmed with fur, or it would have the sleeve styles favoured for the jerkin — loose hanging, with the elbow slit for the arm, or heavily puffed-out with a tight fitting wrist-band. The collar of the shorter gown was of various styles; a large turned back collar tapering in a U to the waist and cut square across the back was very popular, but also used was the high-necked V-throated collar typical of the houppelande.

During the early aprt of the period the cloak was still used as a loose outdoor covering; cut either circular or rectangular it was a traditional garment. In Italy the short cape was worn, hanging down the back to waist level, fastened in front at the throat. Also fastened on one shoulder, these capes were popular in England where they were trimmed with fur edges.

Until about 1520, hose was still made in one piece, either visible right up to the waist or concealed beneath the skirts of the jerkin. After this time hose was split into two parts

54

The lady on the left is wearing
the early sixteenth century fashion of the skirt and bodice being
separate items of attire with full
slashed sleeves. The lady on the
right has the low decolletage
and close fitting slashed sleeves

A man in a short jacket with wide
V-shape opening to the waist
sleeveless with the full sleeves
of the chemise showing. A lady
in the high closed decolletage
and heavy draped skirt long
wide sleeves

56

The gentleman on the left wearing a short gown and a flat hat.
The man on the right with a short
cape hanging on the shoulder
with a tall round hat (late
fifteenth century)

English fashion with a jacket having a wide U-shaped opening to the waist, showing a slashed doublet. Full knee-length skirt. Large slashed sleeves emerging from the just below knee length gown. The gown has a deep fur collar. Low brimmed bonnet hat decorated with ostrich tips. The lady is wearing a low square decolletage with the skirt open showing the decorated under skirt. Large oversleeves fur trimmed and close to the wrist full under sleeves. French hood trimmed with upper and lower billiments

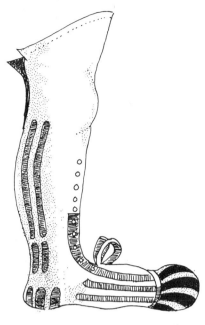

High boot with decoration (late fifteenth century)

known as the upper and nether stocks. The upper stocks were breeches-like garments which varied in length from shorts style to knee-length, and were either tight-fitting or puffed out to various degrees, slashed and decorated to suit individual taste. In Germany, the upper contrasted with the lower stocks and each leg with the other. Indeed, it was in Germany that the upper stocks reached their greatest excesses. Originating with the Landsknechte, mercenary Swiss and German soldiers, the upper stocks would be heavily padded out and liberally slashed to show a brightly coloured lining. Upper and nether stocks would contrast boldly in colour, and even the two upper stocks themselves might be cut in different styles. In other countries, these extremes were rarely met with.

The nether stocks were usually of a knitted material, or still made from seamed cloth or linen, although this was now less popular than it had been in the past. They reached to the knee, or, if necessary, higher up the leg, and were invariably worn with a garter at knee-level or above (sometimes both). The cod-piece, visible beneath the jerkin or gown, was still used with the upper stocks, and was attached to them with buckles or points.

Peasants wore rough separate hose up to the thighs and loose gaiters about the shins from ankle to knee.

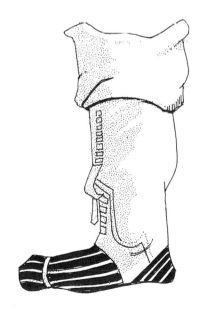

Decorated footwear with sock foot (late fifteenth century)

Footwear   The long-pointed shoe had by now fallen out of fashion and was replaced by a style which was in its way equally exaggerated. Shoes became square-toed, often wider at the toe than for the rest of the shoe. Heels were not used and the shoes, fastened with a strap at the instep, might be without any back at all. These styles were less exaggerated in Italy than the rest of Europe, but in any case became gradually more normal towards the end of the period. Shoe decoration was, like that of the clothes, very flamboyant, adopting slashing to a great extent, the contrast lining being pulled through in a puff from underneath. Jewels adorned both shoes themselves and buckles. Shoe materials included leather, velvet and heavy silks, the more expensive styles adorned with jewels.

Ordinary people and *peasants* used footwear in the same styles, but much less elaborate as far as decoration was concerned. Soft calf-length boots were popular for manual workers; wooden clogs and pattens were also standard wear for peasants.

59

Two dandies of the Italian period in parti-coloured tights (late fifteenth century)

Peasant costume of the early
sixteenth century. The man is
dressed in the short tunic with
shoulder hood and high leather
boots. The woman is wearing
a simple kirtle with a bodice
connected by ties

German and Swiss soldiers with
armour over their slashed costumes

Women's costume　　During this period the flowing line of the houppelande was abandoned and a tight-waisted effect came into vogue. Women's gowns are principally notable at this time for the closely fitting bodices universal throughout Europe, and for the voluminous skirts which trailed around the feet and onto the ground. In Germany, waists and necks were high, sleeves full, whilst in Italy and Spain the waist was lower, and tightly-laced corsets gave a stiff, formal appearance more characteristic of the Elizabethan age.

The high-waisted gown with wide belt and plunging V-neckline was still popular in this period. A newer style,

The woman wearing full draped dress with train and hanging sleeves. Her hair is covered with a kerchief. Rear view of a lady in a high decolletage trained dress with puffed close-fitting sleeves

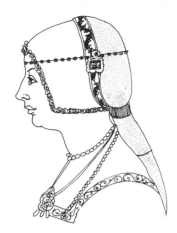

Close-fitting headwear early sixteenth century

Back of the head style beginning
of sixteenth century

The lady on the left wearing a full
skirted trained dress with a
squared neck-line bodice, puffed
sleeves and a high brimmed hat.
The lady on the right with a close
fitting bodice and full trained
skirt, puffed sleeves at the elbow.
High necked decolletage. Built-
up at the back bonnet

Fashionable lady in a low
decolletage close-fitting bodice
dress with close fitting puffed
sleeves with full pleated skirt

High fashion of the early part of the sixteenth century with the separate bodice and over-skirt. The sleeves were close-fitting at the wrist and slashed from the shoulder to elbow and filled with the under-garment full sleeved. The skirt was full and trained

66

Female headwear early sixteenth century

Hair plaited and drawn up onto the top of the head and covered with a fine veil Middle of the fifteenth century

Plain stiffened hood (early sixteenth century)

particularly favoured in Flanders, was a tight, front-laced bodice worn over an underdress which could be seen through the lacings. The bodice of this dress was fitted to skirts either at the waist or at the hips, or the front panel might dip in a deep U-shape over the abdomen, the gown being belted with a wide linked, or woven and braided girdle, perhaps of gold. The skirts were long, and trailing, not open at the front, but were probably lifted in order to show the contrasting skirt or skirts beneath. Close-fitting sleeves were tied to the bodice at the arm-holes and showed the material of the chemise beneath. A decorative slit might be made up the length of the sleeve at the back and laced at intervals, the chemise again showing through. Alternatively, a wide-mouthed full length sleeve or a more moderate elbow sleeve were worn.

Another overdress was a form of sleeveless surcote worn over a front-laced cote and displaying the material of the latter at the neck-line and arm. The surcote displayed a degree of slashing to show off a contrast lining.

The chemise was invariably visible at the neck and sleeves and as in previous periods, is principally important inasmuch as it contrasted with and gave interest to the outer garment.

Later in the period women's dresses took on the squarer look which men's clothing had acquired, this effect being emphasised with broad square or round decolletages at the back as well as the front. In Italy and France a capacious puffed sleeve was favoured, whilst more northerly countries preferred a sleeve narrow at armhole and wrist, but widening to some degree at the elbow.

Women's gowns were usually cut in a large circle, with the result that the waist was considerably smaller in circumference than the hem, which trailed on the ground in a mass of folds. In order to walk unencumbered, women held the bulk of the material gathered up over their stomachs, in a pose frequently seen in the paintings of the period.

Over these dresses women wore a gown with full elbow length or cap-sleeves (for lesser folk) turned back and fur-trimmed. At first it was worn closed all the way round the body, but after 1510 the style for separate bodices and skirts developed. From Italy came the habit of parting the gown front from the waist down, in order to reveal the under-dress. Bodices were back-laced and lay flat over the chest, with a low square decolletage. Skirts were full and

The lady is wearing the German
fashion of a low decolletage and
low back with slashed sleeves
and full trained skirt. The head
is covered with the bonnet
high at the back of the head
with a short veil over the forehead. The soldier figure is
wearing a tight doublet and
hose with the right leg exposed
to the thigh, an Italian style,
and slashed sleeves

Hair encased into horn sheaths (late fifteenth century)

Linen head covering with wimple, late fifteenth century

High brimmed hat (late fifteenth century)

pleated in heavy layers to give a bell-shape to the lower silhouette.

In order to show off their gowns to best effect women wore various extras, particularly false over-sleeves to contrast with the sleeves beneath, and stomachers which emphasised the front-laced opening of the corset. A short shoulder cape often adorned a costume although it was not meant to offer protection from the weather.

Fine ladies could afford to wear long trailing skirts, but peasant women, although they too wore long dresses, hitched them up into belts to facilitate movement. The typical peasant dress was the simple cote with long, moderate turned back sleeves, showing the tight chemise sleeves beneath. A front-laced bodice was typical wear for peasant women.

They might wear a kerchief or collar of white or dark material behind their necks, and a linen bonnet and white apron. For outdoor wear, women wore cloaks in the usual style, frequently hooded.

Long *hair*, worn without any head covering was, as ever, the norm for unmarried girls, particularly, at this time, for brides, and might be adopted by married women too if it was worn with a head covering. This latter practice was particularly favoured by the Italians, who adopted it in a variety of styles. Italian women did not so much cover their hair as decorate it with narrow bands of material or ribbons. Hair was braided or coiled and left to hang in plaits or fastened up on the head. The hair might be centre-parted with a decorated cap or net on top, or worn with a Turban style hat, the hair pulled through the crown and hanging from the neck.

Headdress Women's head-dress throughout Europe assumed a vast range of styles which can only be suggested here. In Flanders the bonnet style was still popular whilst German women favoured the stiffly shaped white linen structures. In England head-dresses were frequently complicated and extravagant, worn with the hair loose or braided up and completely hidden. Particularly favoured at the beginning of the period was the hennin, traditionally associated with women of the middle-ages. It was made from a stiff cone shape extending to a point with a strip of velvet, turned back, framing the face. A length of thin gauze was draped around the cone

Hair close to the face with coiled head-gear at the back. Late fifteenth century

Hair flat to the face and head enclosed in a close fitting cap at the back (late fifteenth century)

Close fitting French hood with fine veil over the forehead (early sixteenth century)

and floated from the tip. The cone was covered with gold or silver cloth, or brocade and velvet, visible through the veil. Another version, the truncated hennin, was of the same structure, cut-off short to give a flat end and not a point. With this style a butterfly veil, radiating out in three wired wings was frequently worn. A jewel might sit in the centre front of the head-dress to set it off. All hair which was visible outside the borders of the cone was shaved or plucked away, although later in the period when head-dresses were worn farther back on the head, this became impossible and a little hair might show at the sides of the forehead. The hennin was worn either fairly upright on the head or slanting farther back. Later in the period the velvet frame of the front of the hennin was worn alone, without the cone. This gave rise, eventually, to a classic English style, the kennel. The kennel was constructed from two units — the front face frame and a veil or drape of material at the back of the head. The frame of the kennel was styled from stiff material and covered with a rich material and at the front of the forehead any visible hair was covered with a roll of striped material or velvet. Simpler styles of the kennel were formed from a close-fitting cap with side pieces which folded back up onto themselves and were pinned up. An extra piece of material might perhaps be draped down at the back of this.

The traditional linen cloth coif was worn in very many different styles throughout Europe, some of which are shown in the illustrations. They ranged from a simple bonnet to the full gorget and wimple which was still the normal wear of religious or pious women. In Germany a particular style was a dome-like stiff structure on linen or a richer material worn alone, or with a white linen coif.

Yet another style was the horseshoe head-dress which curved around the crown of the head and down over the ears almost to the shoulders. The shape was formed from stiff card or buckram, and was covered with velvet or some other such material. A rich ornamentation of jewels or gold-work embellished the material and behind the frame a small cap covered the back of the head. The hair was, in this instance, always visible, centre parted in front of the head-dress. A simple covering used by women in France and Flanders was a wide piece of material laid over the head from back to front over a snug cap extending over each ear and folding back up onto itself. During the early part of the period the

Embroidered 'halo' stiffened hat with snood (early sixteenth century)

Flemish style hood with ribbon lappetts (early sixteenth century)

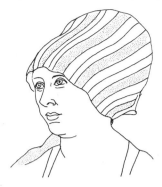

Simple complete head covering bonnet (early sixteenth century)

French hood with upper and lower decoration (middle of the sixteenth century)

heart-shaped and turban styles of the previous era were still popular, and women might generally throughout the period adopt any of the styles of hat worn by men.

The plain linen bonnet was the usual everyday wear of peasants with perhaps a straw hat or peaked hat worn over this.

Shoes were similar to men's being square-toed and of light construction, but they were mainly invisible because of the length of the dresses. Soft shoes decorated with slashes are also typical. Peasant women wore clogs, leather or rush shoes.

Children's clothes   Children were, as always, dressed as their parents, although the complexities of adult dress meant that some simplification was a necessity. Young girls wore a simple bonnet until they were old enough (about ten years old) to adopt more ornate head-dress; boys too, wore the plain bonnet, although they dropped this after infancy.

Jewelled flat hat with feather and jewel-decked snood (early sixteenth century)

Close fitting hat decorated with jewels and feathers (middle of the sixteenth century)

Gable type English hood with pinned up lappets (early sixteenth century)

STAGE PROPERTIES

Helmet known as 'the Great Helm' (fourteenth century)

The bascinet without a visor (fourteenth century)

The conical helmet with a nasal piece (fourteenth century)

When dealing with dramas and pageants of these periods the principal concern of the property department will be to ensure that knights and soldiers appear in the correct armour and with the appropriate weapons. Whilst it is not necessary to cover the subject in intricate detail, it is important that those responsible for the reproduction of armour have an idea of the varieties of protective clothing which were popularly used and the conditions in which they would be worn.

Obviously, it is impractical, from the point of view of both time and expense, for most theatrical companies to be too concerned with the exact replication of weapons and armour but if the attention is directed towards the reproduction of authentic shapes and the suggestion of the correct materials and design, excellent results can be obtained.

In the thirteenth century, and indeed throughout the whole period dealt with in this book, mail was the fundamental item in a soldier's attire. The coat of mail, known as a hauberk, was constructed from a mass of tiny, interlocking metal rings which were carefully assembled to provide a closely fitting knee-length coat. The hauberk usually provided covering for the arms and sometimes the hands, and had a coif of mail to protect the head. It would be slit up to the waist at the front and back in order to facilitate riding.

A padded jacket worn under the hauberk kept its rough surface away from the body. Some knights might wear over the hauberk a tunic of scale armour, made up of small overlapping steel plates covering the torso. Alternatively to this were the gambeson — a sleeveless padded jerkin, the coat of plates, or a leather tunic reinforced with small metal plates.

Whilst most soldiers relied on mail, varieties of plate armour found favour with knights and the few others who could afford it, and by the fourteenth century this became established as a standard form of protection. The use of

The Maid of Orleans in full
armour with her page

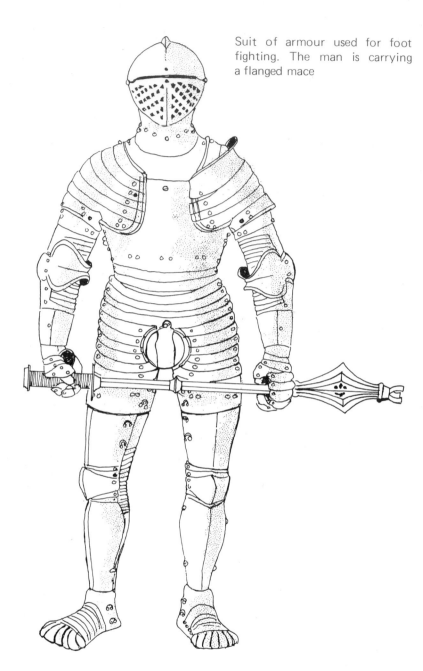

Suit of armour used for foot fighting. The man is carrying a flanged mace

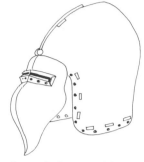

Bascinet helmet with curved visor (fourteenth century)

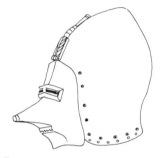

Bascinet helmet with nose shaped visor (fourteenth century)

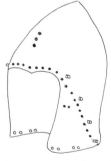

Bascinet without a visor (fourteenth century)

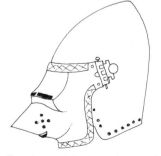

Bascinet with shaped visor (fourteenth century)

plate was at first selective, covering the shins, knees, arms, hands (in the form of gauntlets) and neck, but eventually it came to cover the whole of the body.

When representing soldiers of the thirteenth to the sixteenth centuries all except the knights and, of course, royal personages, can be suitably dressed in the hauberk and mail coif, worn with the gambeson. Suitable helmets are either

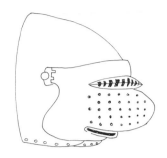

Bascinet with protruding rounded visor (fifteenth century)

The kettle helmet used in many periods (fourteenth century)

Sallet type helmet with neck guard (sixteenth century)

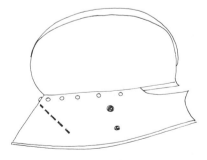

Sallet helmet with a deep neck guard (sixteenth century)

the kettle-hat style or the Norman bowl helmet with a nasal strip to protect the face. The shield (if any) carried by the foot-soldier was the buckler, a small round shield, used in hand to hand fighting.

Knights should be dressed in rather more sophisticated armour: the hauberk with scale armour or a coat of plates. In addition, protective plates can be worn over the legs, arms, neck and hands. The helmet worn by a knight at this time would be either one or other of those already mentioned, or the great helm, a heavy, full face and head cover with slits to see out of, and holes to ease breathing. Over all this went a surcote, or a knee-length tunic of hard leather known as a cuir-bouilli. The king wore the same armour as his knights.

The long kite shield of the Normans was proving to be impractical and by the thirteenth century it had been shortened to take the form which is traditionally associated with the Middle Ages. Slightly convex in shape, it was both easier to handle and aesthetically more desirable, for it was not established practice to decorate the shield and the surcote with the appropriate heraldic device. A knight wearing the great helm would frequently be unrecognisable were it not for the prominent display of his family arms.

At the end of the Early Gothic period and throughout the Late Gothic the increasing skill of the armourer brought about a change in the styles of armour. Plate armour was now more frequently used, and it became normal to cover as much of the body as possible. The commonest plates used were those which protected the lets and knees, arms, shoulders, and later, thighs. The sabaton, or solleret, was worn on the feet. Breast plates fashioned out of a single sheet of metal covered the chest and abdomen, and were either worn with an accompanying back plate, or alone, fastened with straps across the back.

Mail was still the basic part of a soldier's armour, and was worn under the plate armour, often hanging over the thigh where there was little other protection. If plates were not worn the body might be further protected with a tough leather tunic onto which metal rings were riveted.

The greatest changes at this time were in the styles of the helmet. The old bowl-shaped helmet formed the basis for a much finer and considerably more versatile piece of armour, the bascinet. At first the only alteration was an extension of the helmet down over the back of the neck, but this

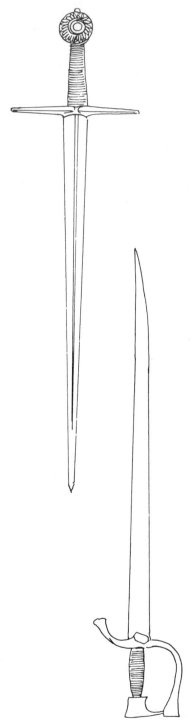

Sword (fifteenth century)

Sword (fifteenth century)

extra protection rapidly extended over the face which had hitherto been particularly vulnerable. The visor, hinged so that it could be pushed up when not required, was initially curved gently over the face, but later was to be seen in a variety of shapes, often with grotesque representations of human features. Protectively edged eye slits, and ventilation holes, are typical features of the visor. The bascinet was not always worn with a visor, and it may be easier to dispense with this refinement, or at least the more elaborate types. The increased protection afforded by the bascinet led soldiers to dispense with the mail coif, and attach a curtain of mail to the back of the helmet in order to protect the shoulders.

The great helm, largely unchanged in shape, gradually fell out of use for the battle-field and was reserved for jousting tournaments. Nor was there much alteration in the shape of the heraldic shield, except that it was now often much smaller.

It is important to remember that armour was very expensive and only the very rich could afford to keep up with the latest designs. More often than not a man would enter the field wearing armour that was neither the best nor the most up to date. In the case of the common soldiers it is quite reasonable to stick to the earlier, simpler types throughout the whole period dealt with here, and when equipping knights it is probably more practical to err in favour of too little armour than too much. Old and new styles would all be seen together and it little mattered what kind of armour was worn, so long as it served its purpose adequately.

The more expensive suits of armour were decorated with edgings of gold, silver and brass, and knights were in the habit of wearing a richly decorated, jewelled sword-belt around the hips. Weapons would often be attached to the breast-plate with chains, so that they might not be lost if they were dropped. Small details such as these, easily reproduced, will give an authentic touch to a production.

During the fifteenth and sixteenth centuries the main development in the manufacture of armour was the degree of sophistication with which it was made. The basic principles remained the same, but shapes were altered as the increasingly professional art of the armourer found more efficient ways to protect the body.

The latest innovation was the armet, a helmet similar to the still widely used bascinet. It was constructed from several plates curved around and in front of the head and

Lady in high-waisted skirt long
and full, the head covered in the
roll shaped headdress. The man
is wearing a suit of armour with
the head protected by a chain
mail hood and the lower part of
the face by the bevore which
reached the nose, he is carrying
the sallet helmet (middle of the
fifteenth century)

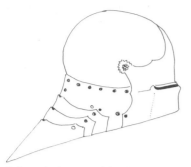

Sallet helmet with laminated neck piece (sixteenth century)

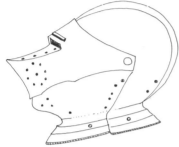

Close fitting helmet with visor (sixteenth century)

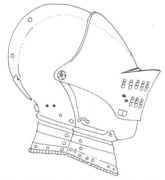

Close fitting helmet with visor (middle of sixteenth century)

Unusual 'Face' helmet Italian style (sixteenth century)

hinged or pinned together. The visor covered only the nose and eyes, leaving a slit which allowed the wearer to see as much as was practical. Occasionally a few gorget plates were attached, covering the throat.

Suits of armour, made mainly in Italy and Germany, were of two distinctive styles — the Gothic, used mainly in Germany, and the Italian, which was popular throughout the rest of Europe. Italian armour was smoothly finished and had a rounded outline which gave it a rather stocky, stable appearance. A lance rest was usually fixed to the breast-plate below the right shoulder. Gothic armour was notable for the quality of the artistic workmanship which was used in its manufacture. It was decorated all over with fluted surfaces and had a characteristic pointed look at the edges. Large numbers of small overlapping metal plates were used to give maximum flexibility. The typical Gothic helmet was the kettle type, or the sallet, which had a long pointed tail to protect the back of the neck. Both Italian and Gothic armour were worn with mail which protected the body where armour was unsuitable; underneath the mail a padded jacket eased discomfort. The use of shields had been generally dispensed with by knights, but two kinds often used by the foot-soldiers were the buckler, probably the favourite throughout this period, and the full, rectangular, convex shield of the bowman which was stood in front of him whilst he fired.

In the sixteenth century the trend towards elaborately made and decorated armour continued, but so complex were these later suits, particularly the Maximilian and Greenwich armours that they are impractical for the purposes of reproduction; most soldiers of this period would have used far less extravagant forms of protection, variations of the Italian and Gothic types, and, doubtless, many of the earlier styles too.

For the most part, the most useful items for a property department to concentrate upon are the hauberk and coif and/or gambeson, with simpler forms of helmet. The various single plates for arms, legs and breast, together with helmet, cuir-bouilli in some cases, surcote, a decorated belt and the heraldic shield will complete the equipment needed for a knight.

By and large, the simpler the armour, the more effective it is likely to look. Complicated suits of armour must be well reproduced if they are to look authentic.

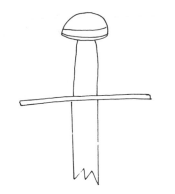

Sword hilt shape (fourteenth century)

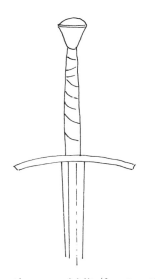

Thrusting sword hilt (fourteenth century)

Arms The weapons available to the medieval soldier changed little throughout the whole period covered here. Such developments as there were were refinements of already well-tried items, and with the exception of hand guns they are more or less universal throughout the middle-ages. The sword was, during the thirteenth century, primarily the weapon used by knights. It was a fairly long, thin-bladed weapon usually with a narrow groove, the fuller, on the flat of the blade from the hilt to within a few inches of the tip. Hilts were normally simply designed, comprising a straight crosspiece, the quillion, and a wooden grip with a more or less round or D-shaped pommel at the end. The sword was primarily a one-handed implement; more rarely it was made with a sufficiently long hilt to allow both hands to be used if necessary. Hilts decorated with delicate gold-work are not representative of the Gothic period; they are more typical of later ages.

An alternative to the common sword was the falchion, a machete-like weapon, designed to deliver a heavy enough blow to cut through armour.

From the fourteenth century onwards a greater variety of swords became available. Thin-bladed thrusting weapons complemented the normal sword which was principally used as a cutting weapon. Blades were lengthened slightly, and pommels increased in size to counterbalance the greater weight.

It was in the fifteenth and sixteenth centuries that ornamental swords appeared. Hilts were decorated in fancy metalwork and in some cases one of the quillions curved up and round onto the pommel to provide a guard for the knuckles. Blade design altered somewhat too; instead of the fuller some blades had a central ridge to give extra strength.

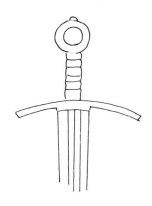

Sword hilt (fourteenth century)

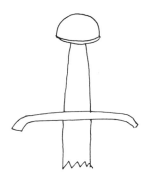

Sword hilt (fourteenth century)

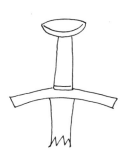

Sword hilt (fourteenth century)

79

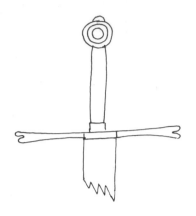

Sword hilt (fourteenth century)

A glaive pole arm (sixteenth century)

Blade lengths varied considerably. By this time the sword had ceased to be solely a weapon used by knights and was used by foot-soldiers as well. When not in use it was carried in a scabbard hung at the left hip from a waist, hip or shoulder belt. The scabbard was made from two fillets of wood bound with leather and finished with metal at the tip and the mouth (chape) which was often decorated with fine metalwork.

In addition to the sword most knights carried a dagger hung from the right-hand side of the sword belt. However, the dagger was only used in combat if it was essential. It had a short, sturdy blade and circular or down-curved quillions. At the time of the Renaissance dagger hilts had come to be very decoratively worked.

Apart from their military use, swords and daggers had also their place in civilian life. Daggers were worn by men from all walks of life, for some method of self defence was desirable. The dagger was either slipped under the belt or hung from it, or might be slipped through two leather loops on the purse. In the sixteenth century the practice of wearing the dress swords was established. These were lighter than swords used in battles — the rapier was one such.

In addition to the sword, both infantry and knights carried other weapons. The humbler foot-soldier might be armed with only domestic implements such as the billhook or the pitchfork which could be put to use in the field, but there were, of course, more specifically military arms. The long-shafted axe (about 125 cm long) had a curved blade with a spike attached; it was a standard weapon up to the sixteenth century, and a short version was carried by mounted riders. Universally popular weapons were the spiked club and the flanged mace, both heavy crushing implements. Fifteenth century knights favoured the pole-axe and the war-hammer. Other arms used from the thirteenth century onwards included pikes, halberds, glaives and lances, all long-handled weapons; pikes in particular were very effective against cavalry. The lance is the weapon usually associated with the cavalry charge and as such is not likely to concern the property master. The halberds and glaives were carried by foot-soldiers and were most useful for piercing armour.

Two weapons used throughout these periods were the longbow, traditionally an English weapon, and the crossbow. The longbow was about two metres long and was carried with a tall rectangular shield, as already indicated. Longbow arrows were kept in a quiver which hung from the archer's belt or simply thrust through the belt loop. Crossbowmen also used a quiver.

Very occasionally, foot-soldiers would make use of the handgun, in its simplest form even as early as the fourteenth century. By the sixteenth century the hand gun was widely used throughout Europe, and traditional suits of armour, which were easily pierced by the ball, became ineffective as a defence.

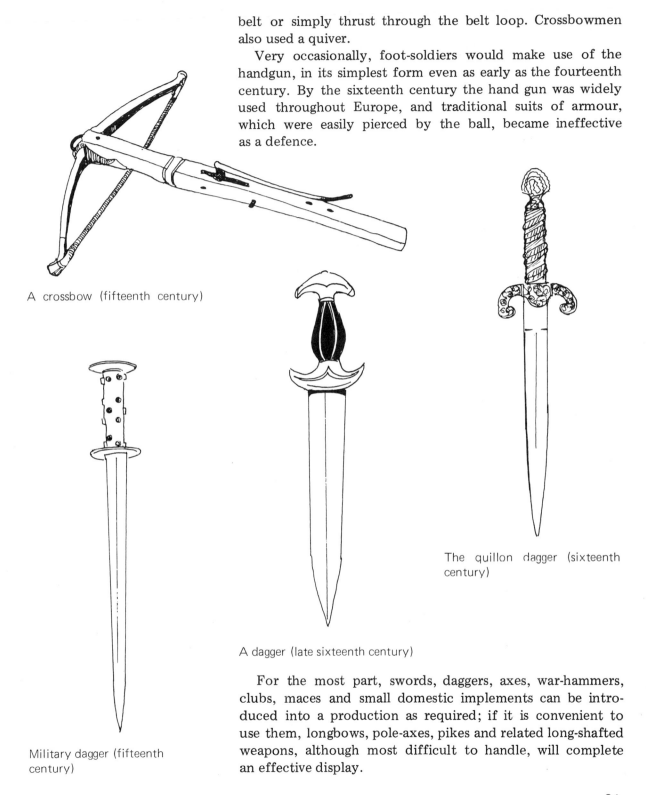

A crossbow (fifteenth century)

The quillon dagger (sixteenth century)

A dagger (late sixteenth century)

Military dagger (fifteenth century)

For the most part, swords, daggers, axes, war-hammers, clubs, maces and small domestic implements can be introduced into a production as required; if it is convenient to use them, longbows, pole-axes, pikes and related long-shafted weapons, although most difficult to handle, will complete an effective display.

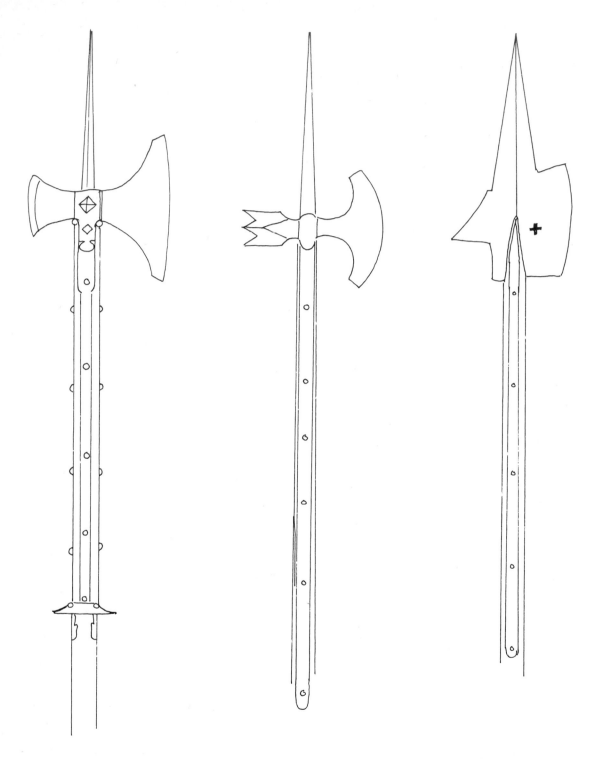

Pole-axe with rondel hand guard
(fifteenth century)

Pole-axe with long spike spear
(fifteenth century)

Halberd with langet
(fifteenth century)

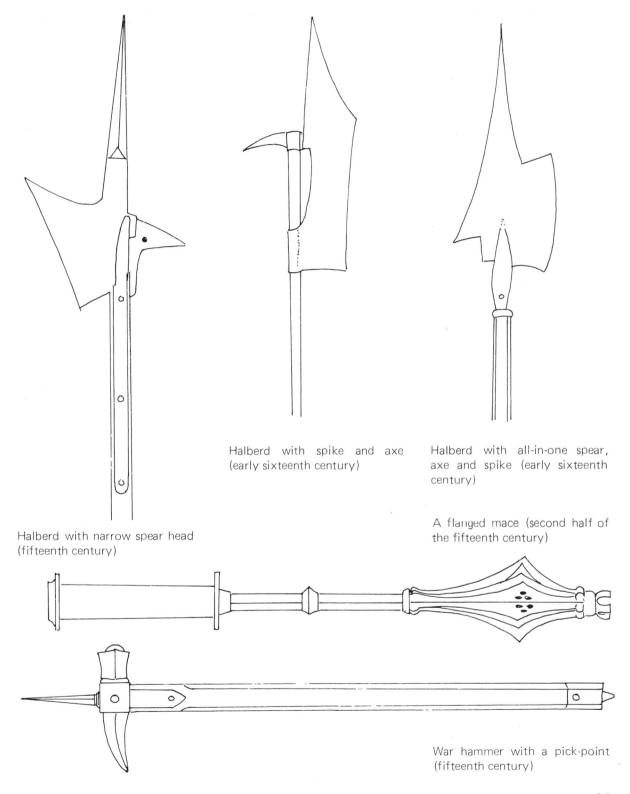

Halberd with spike and axe
(early sixteenth century)

Halberd with all-in-one spear,
axe and spike (early sixteenth
century)

Halberd with narrow spear head
(fifteenth century)

A flanged mace (second half of
the fifteenth century)

War hammer with a pick-point
(fifteenth century)

Country costume of the early sixteenth century. The man is wearing the short tunic with a high cap over his hood. High soft leather boots. The lady is dressed for travelling with hitched-up skirt and hood head-covering

84

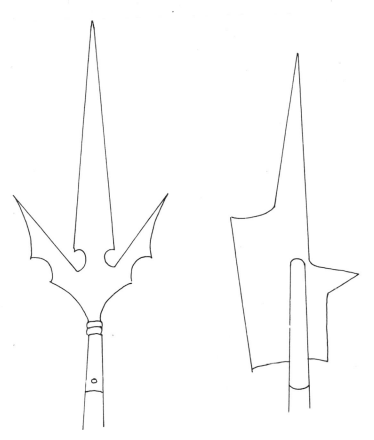

∧ corseque (early sixteenth century)   Halberd (early sixteenth century)

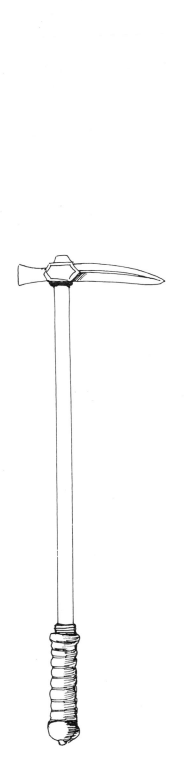

A war hammer (sixteenth century)

Other properties are too numerous to list, and will be determined by the requirements of a particular scene. Some, however, form part of the costume of the times and contribute to the overall setting of a particular drama.

Purses were worn by everyone, attached to the belt, but often hidden beneath the surcote. Travellers and pilgrims often carried large bags, like satchels, on a bandolier; they might also have staves, or, in the case of shepherds, crooks.

In the Late Gothic period the *pomander* came into general use for both men and women. It was a hollow, perforated sphere which contained a perfumed sponge.

Renaissance gentlemen were in the habit of carrying *canes* with decorated knobs on top.

In all these periods *devotional books*, bound in ornamented leather, would often be carried by pious or ecclesiastical personages.

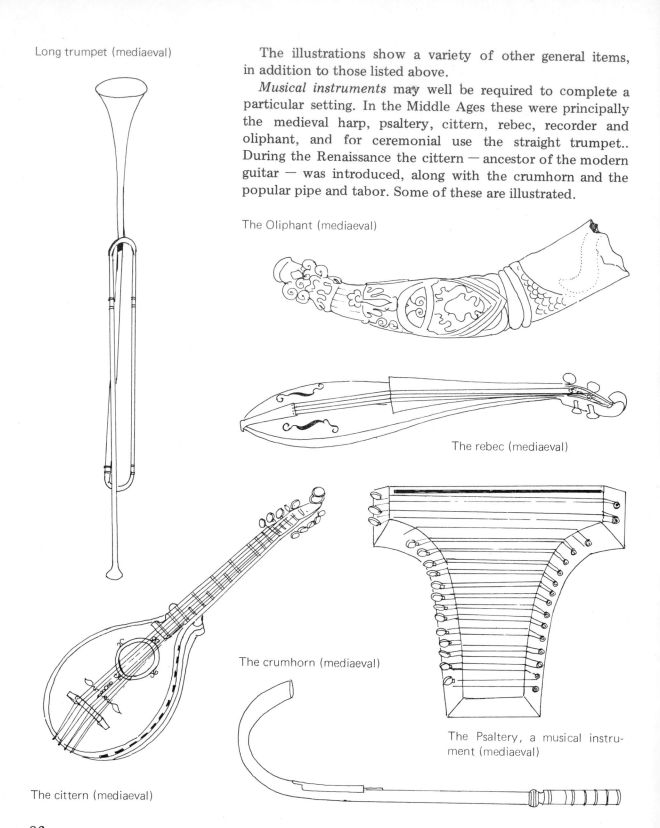

Long trumpet (mediaeval)

The illustrations show a variety of other general items, in addition to those listed above.

Musical instruments may well be required to complete a particular setting. In the Middle Ages these were principally the medieval harp, psaltery, cittern, rebec, recorder and oliphant, and for ceremonial use the straight trumpet.. During the Renaissance the cittern — ancestor of the modern guitar — was introduced, along with the crumhorn and the popular pipe and tabor. Some of these are illustrated.

The Oliphant (mediaeval)

The rebec (mediaeval)

The crumhorn (mediaeval)

The Psaltery, a musical instrument (mediaeval)

The cittern (mediaeval)

SCENIC DESIGN

Successful stage-set designing is not just to be able to visualize the set in its three dimensional form, the stage designer must be able, or have the knowledge and know-how, to construct the set. From the sketches he should be able to build a practical and working stage set keeping to the original design. This task requires ingenuity and inventiveness apart from manual capability.

All stage areas, whether amateur or professional, have a limited space upon which scenery, unless built as a 'standing set', must be able to be moved easily and quickly. Regardless of this limitation of space, the set must be designed and constructed in proportion to the action of the players. So it is important to remember that the scenery pieces must be of a manageable size to be moved by the stage hands and yet be in proportion to the actors. Scene changing is one of the most important factors of any play production; prolonged waits are fatal to any play. If the dramatic flow is interrupted it dampens the enthusiasm and anticipation of audience.

The designer must choose the effect he wishes to create by the set or sets he has visualized around the chosen play. First, there is the realistically painted scene. This must be both well painted and constructed in such a way that it extends impressively out from the stage into the audience. With such a construction there is always a tendency for the eye of the spectator to follow the converging lines and the depth effect of the set to the detriment of the action of the players. For such a background both the producer and designer must have complete and utter faith in their cast and their ability to 'hold' the audience. Nonetheless a realistic setting should tell the audience the whole story and leave nothing to the imagination. Remember that the imitation of nature has its drawbacks if it is too obvious, therefore it is wiser in most cases to be semi-conventional in design.

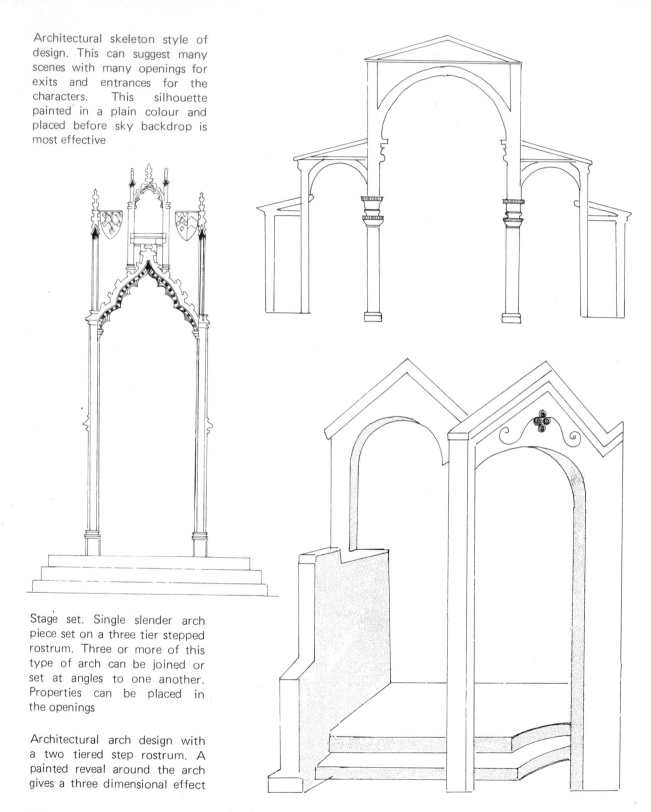

Architectural skeleton style of design. This can suggest many scenes with many openings for exits and entrances for the characters. This silhouette painted in a plain colour and placed before sky backdrop is most effective

Stage set. Single slender arch piece set on a three tier stepped rostrum. Three or more of this type of arch can be joined or set at angles to one another. Properties can be placed in the openings

Architectural arch design with a two tiered step rostrum. A painted reveal around the arch gives a three dimensional effect

The stages in most schools are seldom ideal as they are used for other functions and therefore often present difficulties. Built usually in the older style with a 'proscenium arch' with a removable projecting apron they are a 'hand-down' from the nineteenth-century tradition. With little modification, however, and the use of the latest equipment and modern scenic design, they are ideal for school plays.

As the time factor is very important in most amateur and school productions, settings should be as simple as possible in design and construction. Simple sets still offer great freedom in design and colour. The building and painting of the stage setting is too great a subject for inclusion in this volume. It is an interesting and fascinating subject and the satisfaction of seeing a successful design materialize into a living atmosphere is well worth a greater insight into this activity.

The background to Early and Late Gothic and Renaissance set designing must be studied from the basic architectural appearances of the period. Whether the set is realistic, therefore architecturally correct, a standing set, with rostrums, steps and possibly arched doorways fixed permanently throughout the play, or even a lighted void where light only is used, the success lies in the atmosphere created to represent the period.

Architecture   Domestic buildings of these periods followed closely that of the church architecture: large stone walls and lancet windows, either single or in groups. The doors were large and set in deep recessed mouldings under pointed arches. Fireplaces were simple and shallow, set in chimneys which protruded from the wall. The large stone walls were decorated with tapestries and paintings depicting stories of history and romance. Couches and chairs were covered with silk cushions and draperies. Heraldic devices or banners and shields hung from the rafter beams or upon the walls.

Arcades were now of more slender proportions and pointed lancet arches, at first side by side with round arches of the Norman period, became wider in proportion to their height and were generally crowned with equilateral arches.

The early massive walls remained strongly in evidence but the rough rubble was giving way to the use of cut stones.

Later in the period the inside walls were covered with wooden panelling. The projecting chimney pieces became more ornately decorated.

The Italians favoured fresco-painted walls and ceilings,

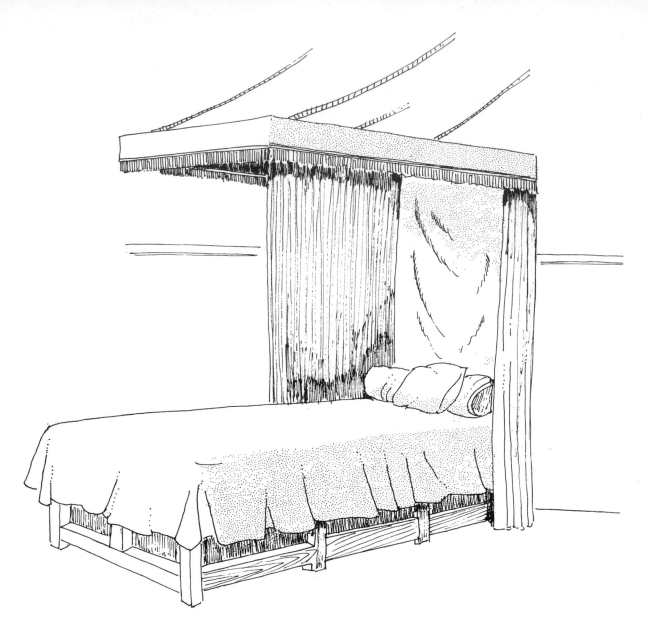

A fourteenth century bed-chamber scene, the bed is a wooden frame with the canopy attached by cords. The side and back curtains are on a running rail attached by rings

and marble patterned floors. A revival of the classical Greek style showed itself in the furniture and decoration.

In designing the set, the properties which decorate the set must also be designed to keep in character with the background. Nothing looks more grotesque than a well-designed set with ordinary modern-type properties added for decoration; they destroy the harmony and atmospheric detail which is so important to the general effect.

The designer must emphasise the properties in his design and their size and colour harmonising with and complement-

Conventional exterior set. This can be used as a central painted set piece or as a cut-cloth (centre arch) with a ground-row backing

Conventional styled set piece used alone with just a sky backing, can, with clever lighting, be the basis of a whole play. Rostrums and steps could be incorporated

A simple flat painted cut-out
or groundrow exterior which
will convey to the audience
the period of the play

A group of tents suggests the
prelude to battle, the after-
math of a battle or even a
battle scene. Highly coloured,
they can convey the richness
which was lavished on tents
of this period

ing the sets. Fine detail is unnecessary and conveys nothing to the audience; the distance between stage and spectators makes it impossible to perceive fastidious details. Concentrate on silhouette, mass and outline.

The *furniture* in the Early Gothic period altered little from the heavy carvings of the Romanesque style. Large high-backed chairs of impressive proportions emphasising the importance of those characters who are seated in them. Such chairs were the symbol of authority and were normally used only by important people. Stools were made in various designs. Officially a person of Royal blood sat on the 'curcule' chair.

Large heavy canopied beds and great wooden carved chests were the usual furniture of the bedroom. The great halls of the castle are best depicted with a raised platform placed at the end of the hall upon which is a long narrow dining table covered with a richly embroidered cloth and laid with large metal plates.

In designing properties as part of the set, the same care and research must be applied whilst they may seem insignificant in the design they make a tremendous contribution to the overall effect.

Panelled walls as a background can be used most effectively for fifteenth century interiors

CHOOSING A PLAY

The drama of the Middle Ages grew up without judgement from a preceding era. It had basically a religious background which slowly developed into definite forms or plays. It was at this period that the Passion, the Mystery and the Miracle plays were performed, first based on the life of Christ and acted by priests in the churches. From there they developed outside the church, and the medieval drama of the theatre began with serious religious plays. The Mysteries were humourous types of play, which included grand profusion of devils.

Although this was an age of great change and fashion especially among the wealthier classes, the medieval drama produced little or no great literature, though it was the beginning of the theatre which was to achieve great artistic heights in the Elizabethan period.

The costumes of this period play a great part in many of Shakespeare's plays and even today the English pantomime follows the tradition of the past and includes many of the medieval costumes mixed with fashions of later centuries.

The following are a few of the productions which can be enacted in the medieval style.

Canterbury Tales by Chaucer
Canterbury Pilgrims by Percy Mackaye
Shakespeare's *King John, Richard II, Richard III, Henry IV, Henry V, Henry VI, Henry VIII, Two Gentlemen of Verona, Merchant of Venice, Romeo and Juliet*
St Joan by Bernard Shaw
Doctor Faustus and *Edward II* by Christopher Marlowe
If I Were King by Justin McCarthy
The Man who Married a Dumb Wife by Anatole France
Many Miracle plays, religious dramas and pageantry.

All good bookshops stock catalogues of plays which give clear details of casts and stage settings.

INDEX

95